WALKI
TO WISDOM

LITERATURE GUIDE SERIES

The Man Born to Be King

Dorothy L. Sayers

by Hannah Eagleson

Inklings Collection

Walking to Wisdom Literature Guide: The Man Born to Be King

Version 1.0
ISBN: 978-1-60051-258-2

Classical Academic Press
515 S. 32nd Street
Camp Hill, PA 17011

www.ClassicalAcademicPress.com

Series Editor: Christine Perrin
Editor: Janet Dixon
Cover Design: Kristin Roach
Interior Design: Lenora Riley & Kristin Roach
Illustrations: Elaine Zubrod

PGP.11.20

Walking to Wisdom Literature Guide: *The Man Born to Be King*

Table of Contents

*An explanation of Dorothys Sayers's inclusion in The Inklings Collection is provided in this introduction to the Inklings.

Introduction to Students

Dear Students,

We are excited that you have the privilege of reading *The Man Born to Be King* alongside a mentor (the writer of this guide) who will lead you "further up and further in" (C.S. Lewis's words in *The Last Battle*). We aim to give you a delightful experience with this book and, in the process, to share practices that we have learned that will help you become a good reader:

- reading carefully
- taking time to absorb a book
- paying attention to details as well as to great ideas over the whole book
- learning to mark up a book
- taking a few notes while reading
- learning to ask and answer good questions
- synthesizing those questions together in a piece of writing or an engaging project

If you spend a year doing all of the Inklings courses, you will not only collect some of the most important books and thoughts, but you will also have increased your abilities and pleasures as a reader.

C.S. Lewis, J.R.R. Tolkien, and Dorothy Sayers (two members and a friend of the Inklings whose work we will study in the Walking to Wisdom Literature Guides: The Inklings Collection) wrote nonfiction as well as fiction, and we begin your reading of fiction with a few select nonfiction essays they wrote on topics that overlap with the topics in the book you are reading. Part of their remarkable legacy is that they wrote about many of the same great ideas in stories, plays, and poems and in nonfiction essays. This means that reading the ideas without the stories in these nonfiction works, or "context essays," will be a significant help to you in understanding them and in fully exploring the characters, plot, and imagery.

We have suggested three reading schedules for *The Man Born to Be King*—one that allows fifteen days to study the book, another that allows twenty, and a third that allows forty days. Feel free to adjust the schedule or add extra time for writing and enrichment activities (found on page 139). Your teacher will know what is best for your schedule.

We have provided you with some space for answering questions, but we recommend that you also keep your thoughts, notes, and musings in a three-ring binder (or on the computer). For the life questions, you may want to keep a separate journal for meditative contemplation. We would like you to have as much room as you need, because you will find that the Inklings writers require a lot of space! It is highly recommended that you look up unfamiliar words found in Dorothy Sayers's *The Man Born to Be King*, and keep a journal of these new vocabulary words and definitions as you work through the book and the guide.

You have the option of studying one guide or a few, or taking a year to study them all to fulfill your British literature requirement for high school English. Enjoy the study!

Scope and Sequence for the Walking to Wisdom Literature Guides: The Inklings Collection

C.S. Lewis

Context Essays* (selections from these are read at the beginning of each guide): excerpts from *Mere Christianity*,[1] *The Weight of Glory*,[2] *On Stories: And Other Essays on Literature*,[3] and "Theology in Stories" by Gilbert Meilaender[4]

- *The Lion, the Witch and the Wardrobe*[5]
- *The Last Battle*[6]
- *The Screwtape Letters*[7]
- *Till We Have Faces*[8]

Dorothy Sayers

Context Essays*: excerpts from *Letters to a Diminished Church*[9]

The Man Born to Be King (twelve-play cycle integrating the four Gospels)[10]

J.R.R. Tolkien

- *The Fellowship of the Ring*[11]
- *The Two Towers*[12]
- *The Return of the King*[13]

*Please note that the context essays are not supplied in this book. In the footnotes on this page we have supplied links that will guide you to where you can purchase or find the context essays. A PDF containing a list of all of the context essays and links to where you can purchase or find them is available at http://capress.link/wtwce01.

1. The Walking to Wisdom Literature Guides: The Inklings Collection is keyed to the following editions listed in these footnotes: C.S. Lewis, *Mere Christianity* (New York: HarperOne, 2009). **Available at https://amzn.to/2ImL1z9.**
2. C.S. Lewis, *The Weight of Glory* (New York: HarperOne, 2009). **Available at https://amzn.to/2Ii9BBa.**
3. C.S. Lewis, *On Stories: And Other Essays on Literature* (San Diego: Harcourt Books, 1966). **Available at https://amzn.to/2KpZXt7.**
4. Gilbert Meilaender, "Theology in Stories: C.S. Lewis and the Narrative Quality of Experience," *Word and World* 1/3 (1981): 222. **Available at http://wordandworld.luthersem.edu/content/pdfs/1-3_Experience/1-3_Meilaender.pdf.**
5. C.S. Lewis, *The Chronicles of Narnia* (New York: HarperCollins, 2001). **Available at https://amzn.to/2Imkan7.**
6. Lewis, *Chronicles.*
7. C.S. Lewis, *The Screwtape Letters* (New York: HarperOne, 2009). **Available at https://amzn.to/2jZrlTv.**
8. C.S. Lewis, *Till We Have Faces* (Orlando, FL: Harcourt, Brace, & Co., 1980). **Available at https://amzn.to/2IL0AA7.**
9. Dorothy Sayers, *Letters to a Diminished Church* (Nashville, TN: Thomas Nelson, 2004). **Available at https://amzn.to/2k0jIfF.**
10. Dorothy Sayers, *The Man Born to Be King: A Play-Cycle on the Life of Our Lord and Saviour Jesus Christ, Written for Broadcasting* (Grand Rapids, MI: Eerdmans, 1943). Reprinted with permission by Classical Academic Press, 2014. **Available at https://classicalacademicpress.com/product/the-man-born-to-be-king/.**
11. J.R.R. Tolkien, *The Fellowship of the Ring* (Boston: Mariner Books, 2005). **Available at https://amzn.to/2jZvEhm.**
12. J.R.R. Tolkien, *The Two Towers* (Boston: Mariner Books, 2005). **Available at https://amzn.to/2Gj7N5c.**
13. J.R.R. Tolkien, *The Return of the King* (Boston: Mariner Books, 2005). **Available at https://amzn.to/2L1JsVa.**

THE INKLINGS

The Inklings was an informal literary discussion group associated with the University of Oxford, England, for nearly two decades between the early 1930s and late 1949.[1] The Inklings were writers, including C.S. Lewis, J.R.R. Tolkien, and Charles Williams, who shared a love of similar stories and a remarkable commitment to ideas they shared. Their literary philosophies tended to depart from the period in which they were writing (modernist, 1900–1950) as did their cultural values. They liked to walk together and meet regularly to read their work aloud to one another.

"Properly speaking," wrote Warren Lewis (brother of C.S.), "the Inklings was neither a club nor a literary society, though it partook of the nature of both. There were no rules, officers, agendas, or formal elections."[2] While Dorothy Sayers did not attend the meetings herself, partly because she didn't live in the same town or teach at Oxford, some have called her an Inkling based on her friendship with Lewis and Charles Williams. Her correspondence with both was avid and their work concerned with many of the same subjects, characters, and plots. They were a great encouragement to one another. Lewis even read Sayers's play cycle, *The Man Born to Be King*, each year during the Lenten period. Therefore, although Sayers was not an "official" member of the Inklings, but rather a close friend of Lewis and Williams, we have included her in the Walking to Wisdom Literature Guides: The Inklings Collection, considering her an Inkling "in spirit," which is to say that she shared the same ideas and aspirations and engaged in similar writing projects. Had she lived in Oxford, we suspect she would have attended the informal meetings of this remarkable group.

Readings and discussions of the members' unfinished works were the principal purposes of meetings. Tolkien's *The Lord of the Rings*, Lewis's *Out of the Silent Planet*, and Williams's *All Hallows' Eve* were among the first novels the Inklings read to one another. Tolkien's fictional Notion Club (see *Sauron Defeated*) was based on the Inklings. Meetings were not all serious; the Inklings amused themselves by having competitions to see who could read notoriously bad prose for the longest without laughing.[3]

Until late 1949, Inklings readings and discussions usually occurred during Thursday evenings in C.S. Lewis's college rooms at Magdalen College. The Inklings and friends were also known to gather informally on Tuesdays at midday at a local public house, The Eagle and Child.

We hope that you will keep the spirit of the Inklings alive in your own study of this guide by working out your own responses to their work in community and conversation as well as laboring over your writing and sharing it with fellow travelers seeking to walk a similar path.

---

1. Clyde S. Kilby and Marjorie Lamp Mead, eds., *Brothers and Friends: The Diaries of Major Warren Hamilton Lewis* (San Francisco: Harper & Row, 1982), 230.
2. Bruce L. Edwards, *Apologist, Philosopher, and Theologian*, vol. 3 of *C.S. Lewis: Life, Works, and Legacy* (Westport, CT: Praegar, 2007), 279.
3. "War of Words over World's Worst Writer," *Culture Northern Ireland*, May 9, 2008, <http://www.culturenorthernireland.org/article/1739/war-of-words-over-world-s-worst-writer?search=inklings&rpg=1>.

Daily Reading Outlines for Dorothy Sayers's *The Man Born to Be King*

With each of the three schedules below, it is very important to read Sayers's introductory notes section before each play. It helps enormously in understanding the importance of each play and its themes. You will find that many of your questions are addressed or answered in these notes by Sayers that explain what she intended.

We have provided a fifteen-day, a twenty-day, and a forty-day reading schedule. While we have estimated the reading time in several schedules to the best of our ability, student reading speeds and classroom goals will differ. The amount of time you will need to complete the writing and discussion work of the literature guides alongside the reading will likely double the amount of time you use. This will vary according to the goals of the teacher and the development of the students. You will also need to add time for essay writing and enrichment activities at the end.

Reading Schedule 1—Fifteen Days

Day 1: Context essay excerpts from *Letters to a Diminished Church:* "The Dogma Is the Drama" and "The Greatest Drama Ever Staged"

Day 2: Context essay excerpt from *Letters to a Diminished Church:* "The Triumph of Easter"

Day 3: Introductory poem "The Makers," and the summary in this guide (page 13) of the introduction to *The Man Born to Be King**

Day 4: Play 1—Notes and *Kings in Judaea*

Day 5: Play 2—Notes and *The King's Herald*

Day 6: Play 3—Notes and *A Certain Nobleman*

Day 7: Play 4—Notes and *The Heirs to the Kingdom*

Day 8: Play 5—Notes and *The Bread of Heaven*

Day 9: Play 6—Notes and *The Feast of Tabernacles*

Day 10: Play 7—Notes and *The Light and the Life*

Day 11: Play 8—Notes and *Royal Progress*

Day 12: Play 9—Notes and *The King's Supper*

Day 13: Play 10—Notes and *The Princes of This World*

Day 14: Play 11—Notes and *King of Sorrows*

Day 15: Play 12—Notes and *The King Comes to His Own*

Reading Schedule 2—Twenty Days

Day 1: Context essay excerpt from *Letters to a Diminished Church:* "The Dogma Is the Drama"

Day 2: Context essay excerpt from *Letters to a Diminished Church:* "The Greatest Drama Ever Staged"

Day 3: Context essay excerpt from *Letters to a Diminished Church:* "The Triumph of Easter"

Day 4: Introductory poem "The Makers," and the summary in this guide (page 13) of the introduction to *The Man Born to Be King**

Day 5: Play 1—Notes and *Kings in Judaea*

Day 6: Play 2—Notes and *The King's Herald*

Day 7: Play 3—Notes and *A Certain Nobleman*

Day 8: Play 4—Notes and *The Heirs to the Kingdom*, scene 1

Day 9: Play 4—*The Heirs to the Kingdom*, scenes 2 and 3

Day 10: Play 5—Notes and *The Bread of Heaven*

Day 11: Play 6—Notes and *The Feast of Tabernacles*

Day 12: Play 7—Notes and *The Light and the Life*

Day 13: Play 8—Notes and *Royal Progress*, scenes 1 and 2

Day 14: Play 8—*Royal Progress*, scene 3

Day 15: Play 9—Notes and *The King's Supper*, scene 1

Day 16: Play 9—*The King's Supper*, scenes 2 and 3

Day 17: Play 10—Notes and *The Princes of This World*

Day 18: Play 11—Notes and *King of Sorrows*, scene 1

Day 19: Play 11—*King of Sorrows*, scenes 2 and 3

Day 20: Play 12—Notes and *The King Comes to His Own*

*Note: You are not expected to read the introduction itself, though it is fascinating and you may enjoy it if you do read it.

Reading Schedule 3—Forty Days

Days 1–2: Context essay excerpt from *Letters to a Diminished Church:* "The Dogma Is the Drama"

Days 3–4: Context essay excerpt from *Letters to a Diminished Church:* "The Greatest Drama Ever Staged"

Days 5–6: Context essay excerpt from *Letters to a Diminished Church:* "The Triumph of Easter"

Days 7–8: Introductory poem "The Makers," and the summary in this guide (page 13) of the introduction to *The Man Born to Be King**

Days 9–10: Play 1—Notes and *Kings in Judaea*

Days 11–12: Play 2—Notes and *The King's Herald*

Days 13–14: Play 3—Notes and *A Certain Nobleman*

Days 15–16: Play 4—Notes and *The Heirs to the Kingdom*, scene 1

Days 17–18: Play 4—*The Heirs to the Kingdom*, scenes 2 and 3

Days 19–20: Play 5—Notes and *The Bread of Heaven*

Days 21–22: Play 6—Notes and *The Feast of Tabernacles*

Days 23–24: Play 7—Notes and *The Light and the Life*

Days 25–26: Play 8—Notes and *Royal Progress*, scenes 1 and 2

Days 27–28: Play 8—*Royal Progress*, scene 3

Days 29–30: Play 9—Notes and *The King's Supper*, scene 1

Days 31–32: Play 9—*The King's Supper*, scenes 2 and 3

Days 33–34: Play 10—Notes and *The Princes of This World*

Days 35–36: Play 11—Notes and *King of Sorrows*, scene 1

Days 37–38: Play 11—*King of Sorrows*, scenes 2 and 3

Days 39–40: Play 12—Notes and *The King Comes to His Own*

*Note: You are not expected to read the introduction itself, though it is fascinating and you may enjoy it if you do read it.

Make Notes: Possess the Book

Becoming a reader is all about learning to pay attention and gather the details to relish and realize the significance and unity of what you are reading. Try using the following symbols or making up your own system that covers the same basics. Underline interesting passages. Write in the margins so that you can go back to reference what you wrote to make your Great Ideas Quotes pages, answer questions, hold discussions, and support points you make in your writing assignments. Here is a simple marking system that we have found effective:

- *   This is important or delightful.
- ?   I have a question.
- ?? I'm confused.
- !   This is surprising or exciting to me.
- T   This could relate to one of the themes or motifs of the book.
- ✓   This relates to something else I have read.
- X   This is part of the conflict or the problem of the story.
- C   This is significant in defining this character.

Tracing the Great Ideas

In each play you will see there are several great ideas chosen for you on which to take notes. (Please remember that you are welcome to find your own great ideas in addition to ours.) As you read, look for and choose quotes related to the given great ideas themes so that you can trace them all the way through the book. Then be on the lookout for how they are worked out in each particular context. Write the quotes in the Great Ideas Quotes sections in each play unit. You may need to add a summary note to introduce the quotes since the plays are comprised almost entirely of dialogue. (See page 17 from the first play for an example of how to record the quotations.) At the end of the guide you will reflect upon the themes of the play and use these quotations to create and support your thesis, from which you will develop an argumentative essay. Each theme will be explained again the first time it appears.

Great Ideas in The Man Born to Be King

Kingship/Leadership

As might be guessed from the title, this play cycle spends a great deal of time exploring the nature of kingship and leadership. It keeps returning to the question of what it looks like to guide or rule people well, especially for someone who holds a political office. It presents several different models not only of how people should rule, but also of how people do rule—that is, *The Man Born to Be King* tries to present a realistic picture of how leadership often works, as well as a model of how it should work.

Kingdom of God

Sayers spends a good deal of time in *The Man Born to Be King* presenting models of how earthly leadership does work and sometimes of how it should work. But more importantly, the play cycle constantly affirms that there is a different and better kind of kingdom, the Kingdom of God. The Kingdom Jesus is leading looks very different from the kingdoms of this world. Sayers draws on the biblical language of the Kingdom of God to flesh out this distinction in the course of the play cycle. In Scripture, Christ is always using metaphor, story, and analogy to describe the nature of the life and world He desires human beings to participate in with Him. He describes this life and world as the Kingdom of God, and uses all sorts of descriptions of it that invite thought and work to understand—it is like a mustard seed, it is like a king having a feast, it is like a merchant buying a beautiful pearl, and so on. Sayers works with this scriptural language to create a sense of God's Kingdom as something centrally important in the play cycle. We will discuss this frequently, so be on the alert for metaphors and stories about the Kingdom.

Prophecy

Prophecy is the prediction of future events. In *The Man Born to Be King* it is an important theme, because God's prophets predicted the coming of the Messiah and many of the things Christ and those around Him would do. Prophecy also ties to the ideas about individual choice and freedom discussed in the essay "The Triumph of Easter." Predictions made by God's true prophets will come true either way, but the individual has a choice about how to participate in them. An individual can freely participate in God's will and have the prophecies come true in a good way in the self; or an individual can fight against God and have the prophecies come true upon the self in a destructive way. The individual has the free choice of how to interact with God and with what He says about the future.

God dying and rising in history

This theme recurs in Sayers's essays, that in Christ all the myths of dying and rising gods come true in the concrete facts of history.

(For some background on how Lewis and Tolkien thought about this topic, read the appendix, titled "Lewis and Tolkien's View on Myth, and Myth Become Fact.")

Pride/Humility

The contrast between pride and humility is one of the most central themes of *The Man Born to Be King*. Pride is the sin that makes someone turn inward toward the self, that makes a person unable to desire things outside the self rightly, even God. Humility is the virtue that allows the self to see its right place in the world, to enjoy belonging to a world wider and greater than the self, and ultimately to enjoy and worship God.

Food/Feasting

Food and feasting is a central metaphor in Scripture, and Sayers frequently uses it in *The Man Born to Be King*. The imagery of food often suggests God's desire to nurture and provide for His people, and feasting brings to mind His longing to celebrate with them. Feasting also often suggests the end of time, when God will renew all things and make a feast for His people.

Christ as human and divine

Sayers emphasizes the importance of Christ's being both God and man over and over in her essays and in the plays themselves. It is the fact that Jesus is both man and God that lets Him bring redemption—if He were only God, He could not suffer human troubles and through that understand humanity and pay the price for our sins. If He were only man, He could not bring about transformation in the human condition.

The transcendent or numinous/The everyday

Throughout *The Man Born to Be King*, there are moments when human beings confront something vastly beyond themselves and are moved, changed, or often completely undone by that thing. They see its beauty and are overpowered by it. This mode of experience often comes from a confrontation with something that is transcendent, such as an angel, or more often in *The Man Born to Be King* from a direct confrontation with the glory of God, the source of transcendence. This kind of astonishing and catastrophic experience of the spiritual world can be described by the adjective "numinous," which comes from a word meaning "spirit" or "god." While other religions and many mythologies have a concept of the numinous or transcendent, in Christian thought this kind of experience stems ultimately from God's glory. There are many moments in the play cycle when someone tries to describe this kind of mysterious and awe-inspiring experience; pay attention to that character as you read. While the experience of the transcendent or the numinous sometimes seems entirely removed from everyday life, the two are often closer than you would think in *The Man*

Born to Be King. Watch for moments when the two appear together and think about what Sayers might be saying about their relationship.

Forgiveness

Forgiveness is the ability to recognize someone else's sin and choose to extend a continued loving relationship to him. Sin functions a bit like debt—if you have sinned against someone, you owe it to him to try to heal the damage that you did. Fundamentally, though, we are not capable of healing the damage that we do to ourselves and the hurt we cause God, and so forgiveness is necessary if we are to have any sort of relationship.

Life/Death

The contrast between life and death is one of the starkest in Scripture and in *The Man Born to Be King*. Beyond physical life and death, the contrast suggests also the difference between spiritual life and spiritual death. Spiritual life is found in a connection to God that allows the human being to flourish and to thrive in right relationship to the Creator of life. Spiritual death occurs when the human being is cut off from God. Because God is the center of all things, to be cut off from Him is to lose everything. If the state of being cut off from God continues, the human being will shrivel as certainly as a plant cut off from its roots.

Blindness/Sight

Sight in *The Man Born to Be King* usually indicates the ability to see things spiritually, to understand the Kingdom of God. Blindness means the inability to see God's Kingdom.

Wit/Humor

One thing Sayers consistently emphasizes in *The Man Born to Be King* is wit and humor, especially the wit and humor of Jesus. She reminds the audience frequently of how clever Jesus is and how much He enjoys laughter.

Freedom/Choice

Individual choices and the freedom God gives to each person are huge themes in "The Triumph of Easter" and in *The Man Born to Be King*. Every human being has to choose whether to participate with God in the act of cultivating His creation or whether to rebel against Him and continue in sin. God can make something good from sinful human choices, but that in no way makes the sin itself good, and the person who continues to participate in sin will be destroyed by it. But God offers human beings a free choice—they can participate with Him or refuse to as they will. That choice is central for Sayers's understanding of human life and for the characters of *The Man Born to Be King*.

Redemption

The theme of redemption, God's ability to make good things out of sinful human choices, is a strong one in Sayers's essays and in *The Man Born to Be King*.

Tell It Back

This is a summary exercise, a method of narrating the plays orally, or "telling it back." It is a wonderful option that allows you to narrate the content of each unit by oral summary—with or without a partner(s). This is a basic element of learning to read that never loses its delight and capacity to delight others. It also helps to develop a strong mental outlining ability and memory.

(Optional) We like it when people make their own illustrations for a book to enter more fully into the lives of the characters. Feel free to do so as you make your way through the book, as a summary exercise for each play, or afterward, when you have finished the entire play cycle. How you feel about the book and what you are able to imagine about the book is part of what it is teaching you. Tolkien himself made drawings for many of his own characters.

Reading Questions

Reading questions encourage close reading of the text by asking comprehension questions. All answers are found in the text.

Discussion Questions

Discussion questions require you to synthesize the main ideas of the text that may be either explicitly or implicitly stated. Your answers to these should explain Sayers's perspective, not your own. Depending on your level, learning needs, or preference, the in-depth discussion questions may be written as short answers (one to two paragraphs), discussed with the teacher/fellow students, or simply read to inspire critical thinking.

Life Questions—Journaling Assignment

Dorothy Sayers took the gospels and developed the story aspect, already present, in them when she wrote *The Man Born to Be King*. As such, we are struck by the characters and the situations in which they find themselves. To read the story of Jesus's life in dramatic form might be a different experience than you have had reading the story as Holy Scripture. It becomes natural to apply the gospels to your own life. After each play, several "life questions" help you reflect on your own personal experiences and examine your own life in light of ideas, events, and characters from *The Man Born to Be King*. You may write informal responses to the life questions in a separate journal.

Write Your Own Discussion Questions

At the end of each section, create two discussion questions that you think would make for good discussion among classmates, friends, and family. These should not chiefly be questions that have a sentence-long answer, but rather questions that would stimulate a longer exchange of ideas. Use our discussion questions and life questions as guides for writing yours.

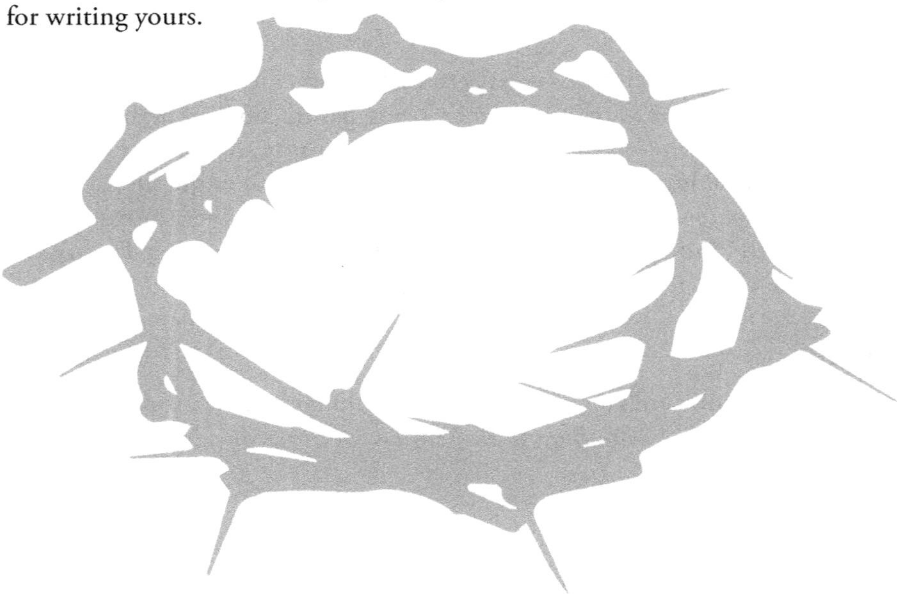

Introduction to *The Man Born to Be King*

Dorothy Sayers forms another link in our Walking to Wisdom Literature Guides: The Inklings Collection. While she wasn't physically present in Oxford during her writing career, she attended Oxford as a student and her work's focus is similar to that of the other Inklings. She also corresponded heavily with C.S. Lewis; hence she has earned a place among the group's members posthumously. The *Touchstone Magazine* article about her (see For Further Biographical Study, page 10), which we recommend you read to prepare for reading *The Man Born to Be King*, describes her as the preeminent Christian female thinker of the modern period. She might not have liked that title, but it is easy to see why she's received it. Her work is varied and runs the gamut from fiction and essays to poems and academic work, including translation. Making good art is the imperative that guided her work; in her experience art that is distinguished for other reasons (other than its artfulness) tends to be lacking in skill.

The Man Born to Be King begins with a poem on making. In her essay "The Image of God" (from *Letters to a Diminished Church*), she writes about the human brain's need for metaphor and analogy to understand things. She explains that we compare what we can't conceive to that which is familiar and claims that we do this in every area of our understanding, including our understanding of God. The creeds (Nicene and Apostles') are the place to which she turns for the metaphors we've received about God. (These creeds declare what Christians believe and were determined by the councils which agreed on the interpretation of Holy Scripture.) God is described as Maker, Father, and Lord. Focusing mainly on God as Maker, she argues that in our capacity to make things (art of all kinds), we draw nearer to understanding God.

How consistent, therefore, that she would follow in the pattern and become a creator herself through plays, essays, novels, and translations. She wanted to fully articulate a dogmatic idea and then roll it into a story to give us access to its dogma through imagination and poetic sensibility. Look at the statements in the poem that support this idea. It talks about the need for mastery in craft and art at the end of this work (8): "Until the dream rise up and stand— / Serve but the stone, the stone serves all" (in other words, our learning to serve, or to craft the stone we are carving, will serve others). Our work here is to labor and "when the greatest and the least / Have finished all their labouring," we will "sit together at the feast, / [and] behold a wonder thing" (8). The wonder we will behold together is God (named "The Maker" in the poem and the creed), and our making comes from His ("Maker of the men that make"). Paradoxically, in the end God Himself will wash our feet and will serve us though we strive to serve Him. Here in this poem her ideas about God as Maker and our own participation in His being and character are compressed.

Reading the gospels as a story acted out with character notes and stage directions makes the sacred narrative newly and powerfully real to us. These sometimes distant figures become characters in our imagination. We enter more deeply into their characterization and even into the unfolding of these remarkable events. We feel the deep pity that good literature elicits. Perhaps we see Judas, for instance, as not simple as we'd imagined—we wonder for a moment that such a thing could have happened to someone who began by standing up so nobly to Baruch. Entering into the gospels as a play might cause us to more readily see various parts of ourselves in different characters. Good questions to ask yourself after reading the play cycle is, "Who do I empathize with? Who am I like?" As the Inklings have taught us in all of their books—self-knowledge is a path to Christ. The play with its wonderful descriptions of characters and lifelike interaction of these men and women in front of us brings this divine reality down to our daily life.

Another example of this divine-to-daily movement is in the character of Mary Magdalene and her loving, giving, desire for union, and deep understanding of Christ as "life." In her character we see that we don't do away with desire when we come to Christ, but instead we learn what is worthy to desire. We find the true source of our desires and are drawn magnetically to Him and away from the twisted, sullied versions of the truth.

But it is also interesting that the play reveals Mary Magdalene's slightly over-dramatic tendencies too in her response to the death of Christ. It does not condemn her or reveal these responses as inauthentic, but reveals the predisposition of her nature. These insights and nuances are infinitely valuable as we attempt to understand the historical and spiritual reality of Christ's presence in this life which is meant to help us live our lives in His.

Flannery O'Connor aptly sums up what I am saying: "Our response to life is different if we have been taught only a definition of faith than it is if we have trembled with Abraham as he held the knife over Isaac." Sayers is offering us the trembling knife to educate and delight our imagination and living knowledge. Come rediscover anew the story you have heard your whole life.

For Further Biographical Study

For a very short biographical introduction to Dorothy Sayers, visit <http://www.sayers.org.uk/dorothy.html>.

For a longer introduction, visit <http://www.touchstonemag.com/archives/article.php?id=13-04-028-f>.

> Note: Parents should first read this excellent introduction to Dorothy Sayers published in a Christian periodical, depending on the age of their child, as it reveals details of Sayers's personal life they may want to save for later. It is in no way graphic or distasteful.

For an introduction to the plays by Gilbert Meilaender through the *Touchstone Magazine* archives, see <http://www.touchstonemag.com/archives/article.php?id=26-02-018-v>.

Summarize the Context Essays: *Letters to a Diminished Church* Excerpts

Before you start *The Man Born to Be King*, you will read and summarize the excerpts from *Letters to a Diminished Church* (sometimes in the course of this guide abbreviated *LDC*) that we have selected. Then cross-check your summaries with ours (in the teacher's edition) to make sure you have covered the topic adequately. Our summaries range from about 90 to 300 words, but your teacher will assign a word count for yours. These "context essays" will help you to understand and gain insight into many of the ideas that arise in *The Man Born to Be King*. An important part of becoming a good reader involves being able to summarize your reading in such a way that someone else can understand what you have read.

"The Dogma Is the Drama" Summary (from *Letters to a Diminished Church*, Chapter 3)

"The Greatest Drama Ever Staged" Summary (from *Letters to a Diminished Church*, Chapter 1)

"The Triumph of Easter" Summary (from *Letters to a Diminished Church*, Chapter 10)

"Introduction" to *The Man Born to Be King* Summary (*We will do this one for you!*)

This is a fascinating and complicated essay, well worth exploring in more depth than is possible here. For this guide, the most important thing to know is the following: the essay explores the challenges and opportunities a playwright faces in telling the story of Christ in a way that emphasizes its historical reality and its dramatic power. If "The Greatest Drama Ever Staged" says that the story of the God who died and rose again in history is an immensely compelling drama, then the introduction to *The Man Born to Be King* describes what it's like to be a playwright trying to make a literal drama out of that material. Sayers emphasizes the inherent drama of the material and its power as a story. She also emphasizes the way that power is even greater because of the historical reality of the events involved, and discusses the challenge of getting across a sense of both story and history.

Sayers wants to make the history feel alive, to get across the drama of the story, and so she translates some historical elements into detail that would make sense to her audience. For instance, to get across the idea that Matthew's social position as a tax collector would have been seen as low, she gives him a Cockney accent, which would have seemed less than refined to her initial audience (see pp. 15 and 34 for notes on Matthew, which will be fleshed out further as you read more of the plays).

Because Sayers has that sense of story and history, this play cycle is a practical working out of an idea you have already met in Sayers's essays and perhaps also in the works of J.R.R. Tolkien and C.S. Lewis. Tolkien and Lewis are fascinated by the idea that in Christ a widespread myth of a god who dies and rises again becomes historical fact. Many mythologies have a story of a god who died and rose from the dead—Odin dies for wisdom while hanging from the World Tree and then rises in Norse mythology, and Osiris dies and rises from the dead in Egyptian myth. Tolkien and Lewis believed this idea was deeply important to human beings and was found in so many mythologies because humanity was hoping somehow, even without knowing it, for Christ. When this myth comes true in Christ's death and resurrection, a deep human need is answered. Sayers emphasizes this in "The Dogma Is the Drama" and "The Greatest Drama Ever Staged." *The Man Born to Be King* is a practical dramatic working out of this idea. It tells the story of Christ as a drama, but one that is keenly attuned to both the mythic resonances of the story and the historical reality of it.

Play 1

Kings in Judaea

Make Notes in Your Book*

Don't forget to make notes in your book!

Tracing the Great Ideas*

Remember, as you read, to look for and choose quotes related to the given great ideas themes so that you can trace them all the way through the book. (Please remember that you are welcome to find your own great ideas themes in addition to ours.) Record them and their page numbers in the space provided in each chapter. You may need to add a summary note to introduce the quotes since the plays are comprised almost entirely of dialogue. Then be on the lookout for how they are worked out in each particular context. At the end of the guide you will use these quotes to create a thesis, from which you will develop an argumentative essay. If you are having trouble knowing which kinds of quotes would be appropriate under the given theme, ask your teacher or consult the teacher's edition.

Great Ideas Quotes throughout the play for the theme *Kingship/Leadership*

As might be guessed from the title, this play cycle spends a great deal of time exploring the nature of kingship and leadership. It keeps returning to the question of what it looks like to guide or rule people well, especially for someone who holds a political office. It presents several different models not only of how people should rule, but also of how people do rule—that is, *The Man Born to Be King* tries to present a realistic picture of how leadership often works, as well as a model of how it should work.

Example quotes

The way the Magi relate to Herod: "Sir, when we have found the Christ—" (41)

Herod lies to the Magi: "May I rely on you to bring me news at once?" (41)

The way the Magi relate to Christ: "Hail, Jesus, King of Heaven!" (44)

Herod's conversation with Proclus about slaughtering the children. (51–52)

*You'll see these icons at the beginning of each unit as reminders to make notes, trace great ideas, and tell back what you've read.

Great Ideas Quotes throughout the play for the theme *Kingdom of God*

Sayers spends a good deal of time in *The Man Born to Be King* presenting models of how earthly leadership does work and sometimes of how it should work. But more importantly, the play cycle constantly affirms that there is a different and better kind of kingdom, the Kingdom of God. The Kingdom Jesus is leading looks very different from the kingdoms of this world. Sayers draws on the biblical language of the Kingdom of God to flesh out this distinction in the course of the plays. In Scripture, Christ is always using metaphor, story, and analogy to describe the nature of the life and world He desires human beings to participate in with Him. He describes this life and world as the Kingdom of God, and uses all sorts of descriptions of it that invite thought and work in order to understand—it is like a mustard seed, it is like a king having a feast, it is like a merchant buying a beautiful pearl, and so on. Sayers works with this scriptural language to create a sense of God's Kingdom as something centrally important in the play cycle. We will discuss this idea frequently, so be on the alert for metaphors and stories about the Kingdom.

Great Ideas Quotes throughout the play for the theme *Prophecy*

Prophecy is the prediction of future events. In *The Man Born to Be King* it is an important theme, because God's prophets predicted the coming of the Messiah and many of the things Christ and those around Him would do. Prophecy also ties to the ideas about individual choice and freedom discussed in the essay "The Triumph of Easter." Predictions made by God's true prophets will come true either way, but the individual has a choice about how to participate in them. An individual can freely participate in God's will and have the prophecies come true in a good way in the self; or an individual can fight against God and have the prophecies come true upon the self in a destructive way. The individual has the free choice of how to interact with God and with what He says about the future.

Tell It Back*

Do an oral summary of your reading on a recording device or to another human being. Narrate the most important events in order while sharing the elements of the characters' development that are important.

Reading Questions

1. In the last section of the notes to this play, Sayers discusses technical issues related to making the play work in the medium of radio (33–34). Choose one of these technical issues and discuss what you would do about it if you were producing the play. Explain your reasoning.

2. Herod orders Proclus to kill the male children under two around Bethlehem, and Proclus refuses. Why does Proclus refuse to kill the children?

   To expand this question: Look at the discussion between Herod and Proclus (51–52). What does this conversation tell you about how each of them sees the world? You may also wish to consult the notes section before the play in order to have more context for the characters of Herod and Proclus.

3. On pages 44–45, the Wise Men speak to Mary about the incredibly difficult questions faced by humanity, and by the Magi particularly as earthly rulers trying to lead well. It is clear from their words that each of them feels keenly the weight of his question. Caspar says, "And the riddle that torments the world is this: Shall Wisdom and Love live together at last, when the promised Kingdom comes?" Melchior goes on to ask, "Shall Power and Love dwell together at last, when the promised Kingdom comes?" Balthazar then continues, "Shall Sorrow and Love be reconciled at last, when the promised Kingdom comes?" What is Mary's answer, which addresses all their questions at once?

4. Why does Sayers have the baby Christ reach out to grab the myrrh offered Him by the Magi?

5. Look at the rhetoric (50) of the speech Herod gives to the people who are trying to remove the golden eagle from the Temple. Identify a few examples of irony in the speech. Irony is found when the apparent meaning of the language is contradicted by the actual situation. (An example would be if something inconvenient happens and someone says, "Great" sarcastically.)

Discussion Questions

1. This play cycle is called *The Man Born to Be King*, and eight of the individual plays refer to royalty in their titles. The first play is called *Kings in Judaea*. We meet a number of kings in the course of the play, offering different models for kingship. How would you describe the difference between Herod's model of kingship and that of the Magi?

   Note: Each discussion question entertains a theme from the course. For the first play we identify the theme, but after that it will be noted only in the teacher's edition

   Theme: Kingship/Leadership

Tolkien and the Means and Ends

King Herod here says, "But which is worse? To kill a score or so of peasant children or to plunge a whole kingdom into war?" (52). He suggests that if the end is important enough—preventing war in a whole kingdom—then the means is justified, however terrible. Sayers clearly critiques that view through the character of Proclus, who refuses to carry out Herod's order, and through the characters of the Wise Men, who seek justice and wisdom in their ruling.

For Tolkien as well, the means never justify the ends. Tolkien's wise characters, such as Gandalf, Galadriel, and Aragorn, are tempted to take the Ring and try to impose goodness by force. But each turns away from the temptation, knowing that any good brought about by evil means will be corrupted and turn evil itself. Good requires good means as well as good ends.

2. One overarching theme of the play cycle is prophecy—the ways that it comes true, the ways that it affects individual lives, the ways that people respond to its fulfillment with joy, dismay, a sense of irony, etc. Choose one moment in this play that includes a prophecy (a foretelling of an event to come) and describe how the different characters in the scene respond to it.

Theme: Prophecy

Life Questions—Journaling Assignment

Feel free to respond to the life questions here or to keep them in a separate journal used for meditative contemplation.

1. Have you been in a situation in which you had to choose between love and what was practical (or pragmatic)? Did your choice threaten to hurt your status or situation? How did you handle it? Do you identify with Proclus or not?

2. Why is it hard to reconcile power and love? Think of someone in your life who is both loving and in a position of power (a doctor, a parent, a teacher). What do you think it must feel like for that person to balance their love with their role of power? Have you ever been in a situation in which someone in that position abused her power and trampled the possibility of love? What did it feel like?

Write Your Own Discussion Questions

1.

2.

Play 2
The King's Herald

Make Notes in Your Book

Tracing the Great Ideas

Record quotations and their page numbers related to the great ideas themes below while you read, and use this page to help you answer the questions that will follow. Remember that all the discussion questions are keyed to the themes of the play.

Great Ideas Quotes throughout the play for the theme *God dying and rising in history*

This theme recurs in Sayers's essays, that in Christ all the myths of dying and rising gods come true in the concrete facts of history.

Great Ideas Quotes throughout the play for the theme *Pride/Humility*

The contrast between pride and humility is one of the most central themes of *The Man Born to Be King.* Pride is the sin that makes someone turn inward toward the self, that makes a person unable to desire things outside the self rightly, even God. Humility is the virtue that allows the self to see its right place in the world, to enjoy belonging to a world wider and greater than the self, and ultimately to enjoy and worship God.

Reading Questions

1. At the beginning of this play, a family with two children named Isaac and Miriam are going to hear John the Baptist preach. When they cross the river, what do the children say?

   To expand this question: What broader significance might their observation have for the audience in the context of the whole play?

2. One of the pleasures of this play cycle is the way that Sayers paints very ordinary interactions among people as well as the moments when everyday life intersects with the extraordinary. Look at the section in which Jesus meets Miriam and Isaac and talks with them (64–65). Do you find the interactions here believable? Do they remind you of your own siblings or of other children you know? Why or why not?

3. Sayers places the parable of the Kingdom coming like leaven in the context of a discussion about earthly power, springing from a conversation about Satan's temptation in the wilderness. Here is some of the context (73):

SIMON: Master, if I understand you right, there's no way by which a man may win power and not become corrupted. But if it's as you say, how is the Kingdom to be restored?

JESUS: I will tell you what the Kingdom is like. You've watched your wife making bread. She takes a little piece of yeast and stirs it into a mass of dough. Then she sets it aside and the buried yeast begins to work in silence and unseen, till the heavy lump rises and swells and becomes light and ready for baking. That is how the Kingdom will come.

The metaphor of the Kingdom coming like yeast in bread tells us several things about the Kingdom. List as many of these ideas that come from the metaphor as you can think of.

To expand this question: Consider the images and the language Sayers uses to make a dramatic interpretation of yeast in bread here. What does this imagery suggest to you? Explore what they might suggest about the Kingdom of God.

Tolkien and Lewis also emphasize the great need for humility and the great dangers of pride. Lewis says in "The Great Sin," an essay from Mere Christianity, "According to Christian teachers, the essential vice, the utmost evil, is Pride. . . . It was through Pride that the devil became the devil: Pride leads to every other vice: it is the complete anti-God state of mind" (MC, 121–122). He goes on to explain that pride is the vice that wants to be the best, and never wants anything superior to the self to exist. He explains how this means that the proud cannot know God, since unless you realize that God is immeasurably superior to the self, you do not know Him at all: "A proud man is always looking down on things and people: and, of course, as long as you are looking down, you cannot see something that is above you" (MC, 124). In Tolkien, the great characters cannot carry the Ring, because they know that it will tempt them to pride in their own abilities and lead them into evil. Many of the characters who have become evil, such as Sauron, became that way through pride.

In Tolkien and Lewis, the dangers of pride are contrasted with the value and the pleasure of humility. The characters who are truly humble are a delight—one thinks of Sam, who is wise in his own quiet way and deeply endearing, or of the good characters in Narnia and their ability to completely lose sight of themselves in their enjoyment of Aslan's goodness.

4. Many people in Jesus's time expected the Messiah to come with great power, to throw the Romans out of Israel, and to establish an earthly kingdom. They expected signs and wonders and political and military strength. In scene 2, sequence 3, how are the disciples showing that they might have expected that, and how is Jesus challenging that expectation? Answer one or both parts of the question.

Discussion Questions

1. In this play, John the Baptist is asking his disciples to read Isaiah 53 when he realizes that Jesus is the Messiah. They are reading it when they see Jesus walking past, and some of them go to find him. Why does Sayers choose this passage as the context for the moment when John's disciples start to realize who Jesus is?

2. Throughout these plays, pride and humility recur as central themes. This play is the first one that includes Judas as a character. In the introduction, Sayers says that she chose to imagine Judas as a man with amazing potential but also with the sin of pride. She writes:

> The worst evil in the world is brought about, not by the open and self-confessed vices, but by the deadly corruption of the proud virtues. Pride, which cast Lucifer the Archangel out of Heaven and Adam out of the Eden of primal innocence, is the head and front of all sin, and the besetting sin of highly virtuous and intelligent people. Jesus, who dealt gently with "publicans and sinners," was hard as nails about the lofty-minded sins; He was a consistent person, and if He spoke of Judas with almost unexampled sternness, it is likely that the sin of Judas was of a peculiarly over-weening loftiness. (22)

Review the notes sections on Judas for *The King's Herald* (56), and what he does in this play. How does Sayers begin here to flesh out the character of Judas, showing the audience both the potential for good and the pride that will corrupt it?

3. There is a point in this play when Judas is making fun of John the Evangelist for getting so enthusiastic about things that he doesn't know what to do, and James says, "Never mind them, John. You have the rare gift of humility—and that's more than can be said of you, Judas, or of most of us" (66). How does Sayers's portrayal of John in contrast to Judas expand your understanding of the contrast between pride and humility?

Life Questions—Journaling Assignment

Feel free to respond to the life questions here or to keep them in a separate journal used for meditative contemplation.

1. In what ways do you identify with Judas? What are the areas of pride in your life?

2. What is a metaphor (a comparison between two things that are very different from each other but strangely help to explain each other) for the way the Kingdom of God has worked in your life? One of the examples in this section is yeast in dough, but your metaphor can be anything—it doesn't have to be biblical. In fact, it will make more sense to you if the metaphor comes from your own life.

Write Your Own Discussion Questions

1.

2.

Play 3

A Certain Nobleman

Make Notes in Your Book

Tracing the Great Ideas

Great Ideas Quotes throughout the play for the theme *Kingdom of God*

This theme recurs in Sayers's essays, that in Christ all the myths of dying and rising gods come true in the concrete facts of history.

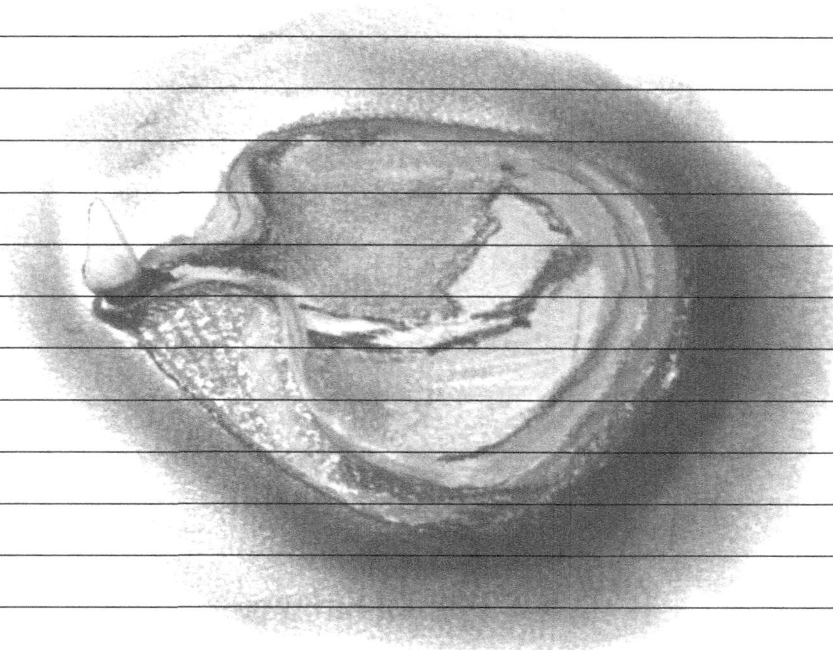

Great Ideas Quotes throughout the play for the theme *Food/Feasting*

Food and feasting is a central metaphor in Scripture, and Sayers frequently uses it in *The Man Born to Be King*. The imagery of food often suggests God's desire to nurture and provide for His people, and feasting brings to mind His longing to celebrate with them. Feasting also often suggests the end of time, when God will renew all things and make a feast for His people.

Great Ideas Quotes throughout the play for the theme *Christ as human and divine*

Sayers emphasizes the importance of Christ's being both God and man over and over in her essays and in the plays themselves. It is the fact that Jesus is both man and God that lets Him bring redemption—if He were only God, He could not suffer human troubles and through that understand humanity and pay the price for our sins. If He were only man, He could not bring about transformation in the human condition.

Reading Questions

1. In this play Mary realizes that Christ is not only human but divine. What does she say and feel about that?

2. One of the great pleasures of reading Sayers is that she frequently lavishes detail on even very minor characters, making them come to life even if they appear only in one play. Choose one of the minor characters in this play and describe one to three things that make that character compelling.

3. In scene 2, sequence 1, Benjamin hears stories of the Prophet, Jesus of Nazareth, and how He has turned water into wine and cleared the Temple. Scene 2, sequence 2, begins with Jesus reassuring the disciples that God will take care of them. (Sayers uses language from the Sermon on the Mount in this scene.) The dialogue runs:

> JESUS: Take all your troubles to God. Ask, and it shall be given to you; seek, and you will find; knock, and all doors will be opened to you. If one of your sons were to ask you for bread, would you give him a stone? If he asked you for fish to eat, would you give him a snake? What do you say, Simon?
>
> SIMON: No, Master. I'm always ready to give my boys anything that's good for them. (94)

What happens next in the play and how does it tie both sequences together?

Discussion Questions

1. Look at the details of how the cleansing of the Temple is presented. What do they suggest about the Kingdom?

2. Please summarize the parable of the lamps in a sentence or two (86). Why does Sayers place the parable of the lamps here? In the context, what does this parable say about the Kingdom of God?

Not a Tame Lion

While Sayers often shows the kindness of Jesus, she also shows His fierce commitment to justice. This scene is much like the reminders in Narnia that Aslan is wild, not like a tame lion (The Chronicles of Narnia, 194). As a symbol of Christ, Aslan is fierce and dangerous, though also very good. This moment of dialogue between Lucy and Mr. Beaver gets the idea across:

> "Then he isn't safe?" said Lucy.
> "Safe?" said Mr. Beaver; "don't you hear what Mrs. Beaver tells you? Who said anything about safe? 'Course he isn't safe. But he's good. He's the King, I tell you." (Chronicles, 146)

3. Mary says, "For He fills the hungry with good things" after Jesus turns the water into wine. Why do you think Mary remembers this line from the Magnificat (scriptural song that she sings when she is told she will bear the Christ in Luke 1:46-55) at the wedding? Discuss what it might imply about Christ in this context.

Life Questions—Journaling Assignment

Feel free to respond to the life questions here or to keep them in a separate journal used for meditative contemplation.

1. Consider Mary's response to Christ's divinity and what that means to her as a mother. Put yourself in her shoes and imagine what that must have felt like. Write a short poem in Mary's voice; feel free take some of the words from the passages in which she speaks.

2. Have you watched the film *Babette's Feast*? Consider a feast you have experienced, perhaps not as grand, but where the good food, fellowship, love, and conversation around the table made you realize something about yourself, life, or God. Describe it.

Write Your Own Discussion Questions

1. ______

2. ______

Play 4

The Heirs to the Kingdom

Make Notes in Your Book

Tracing the Great Ideas

Great Ideas Quotes throughout the play for the theme *The transcendent or numinous/The everyday*

Throughout *The Man Born to Be King*, there are moments when human beings confront something vastly beyond themselves and are moved, changed, or often completely undone by that thing. They see its beauty and are overpowered by it. This mode of experience can come from a confrontation with something that is transcendent, such as an angel, or more often in *The Man Born to Be King*, from a direct confrontation with the glory of God, the source of transcendence. This kind of astonishing and catastrophic experience of the spiritual world can be described by the adjective "numinous," which comes from a word meaning "spirit" or "god." While other religions and many mythologies have a concept of the numinous or transcendent, in Christian thought this kind of experience stems ultimately from God's glory. There are many moments in this play cycle when someone tries to describe this kind of mysterious and awe-inspiring experience; pay attention to that character as you read. While the experience of the transcendent or the numinous sometimes seems entirely removed from everyday life, the two are often closer than you would think in *The Man Born to Be King*. Watch for moments when the two appear together, and think about what Sayers might be saying about their relationship.

Great Ideas Quotes throughout the play for the theme *Pride/Humility*

Great Ideas Quotes throughout the play for the themes *Christ as human and divine, God dying and rising in history*

Reading Questions

1. It's clear that Matthew recognizes from very early on that Jesus knows things about him—things that Matthew is ashamed of. Why does Matthew follow Jesus instead of hiding from Him?

2. In this play, both Peter and Matthew tell the stories of how they first began to recognize who Christ is. This is also the play in which Judas first comes to Christ as a disciple. How does Judas's recognition of who Christ is contrast with the moments recounted by Peter and Matthew? See pages 105–106, particularly the conversation beginning with Judas saying, "Master, I have loved John" and ending with Jesus saying, "I must be alone for a little."

3. How would you perform the following speech from Proclus? If you are in a group, you may wish to take turns reading it aloud and then discuss particularly effective moments of the reading.

> Sir, I have only to look at you. I know authority when I see it. I've been a soldier all my life. I've had to obey my colonel, and my men have had to obey me. I say to the corporal, "Come here", and he comes, and to another man, "Go there", and he goes; or I tell my batman, "Do this", and he does it. And I know very well that when *you* command, you are obeyed. (116)

Discussion Questions

1. As we mentioned in The transcendent or numinous/The everyday theme definition, throughout *The Man Born to Be King*, there are moments when human beings confront something vastly beyond themselves and are moved or changed or completely undone by that thing. Usually in the play cycle, that experience of the transcendent is directly tied to an experience of Jesus or of the glory of God in some other form. One way of describing this experience is found in Sayers's notes on Simon Peter. Sayers describes how Peter has sudden flashes of insight. She notes that the moment when Peter talks about the miraculous catch of fish is like this: "It was just an astonishing catch of fish—and suddenly it came over him that he was a very ordinary sinful man faced with something so beautiful as to be quite unbearable" (99). If you were acting Peter, how would you try to convey that idea in your voice and in how you said the lines given to him on pages 106–107 (beginning, "I remember the very first time I realised" and ending, "that he wasn't ordinary")? If you want, try speaking the lines several different ways. If you're in a group, maybe more than one of you would like to try it.

2. Sayers says of Judas:

> He is passionately sincere. He means to be faithful—and he will be faithful—to the light which he sees so brilliantly. What he sees is the true light—only he does not see it directly, but only its reflection in the mirror of his own brain; and in the end that mirror will twist and distort the reflection and send it dancing away over the bog like a will o' the wisp. He has all the gifts—both the practical and imaginative; and his calculating friend the Zealot is quite right in saying that he will fall, like Adam, by the sin of spiritual pride. He could have been the greatest in the Kingdom of Heaven, but he will be the worst—the worst that is the corruption of the best. (100–101)

Look at the way Jesus and Judas interact when Judas comes to join the disciples (105–106). Jesus recognizes Judas's gifts, and then asks, "Can you be faithful?" Judas answers, "I hope so. I will tell you this; if I set my hand to the plough, I will never look back, though the furrow should run with tears and blood." Jesus replies, "That, I am sure, is true. Take care lest it turn out truer than you think" (106).

Committing wholly to something and refusing to look back through great suffering is usually a praiseworthy thing. Why does Jesus warn Judas about its potential dangers here? Keep in mind the passage above from the notes as you think about the answer.

3. We've been following the theme of God entering history as a man. How does Proclus provide another way of approaching this theme?

Life Questions—Journaling Assignment

Feel free to respond to the life questions here or to keep them in a separate journal used for meditative contemplation.

1. Has someone you respected discovered something embarrassing or even shameful about you and still liked you? What did it feel like? How did you feel about that person? How did you feel about yourself?

2. Have you ever encountered an event or small happening that caused you to remember Christ's presence in the moment with you (which you had forgotten)? Describe it.

Write Your Own Discussion Questions

1.

2.

Play 5
The Bread of Heaven

Make Notes in Your Book

Tracing the Great Ideas

Great Ideas Quotes throughout the play for the theme *Food/Feasting*

Great Ideas Quotes throughout the play for the themes *Kingship/Leadership, Kingdom of God*

Great Ideas Quotes throughout the play for the theme *Pride/Humility*

Tell It Back

Reading Questions

1. At the end of scene 2, after a very busy day for the disciples, Jesus guesses rightly that Peter has been grumbling. When Peter admits to it and apologizes, Jesus tells the parable of the man with two sons. One says he will go and work on his father's land very cheerfully but gets distracted and doesn't do it. The other one grumbles and says that he won't do it, but then has a change of heart and goes to do the work. At the end of the story, Jesus asks: "Now which of those two did the will of his father? . . . It doesn't need an answer, does it?" (133). What does placing this parable here suggest about Sayers's interpretation of Jesus?

2. The way that Judas describes the teaching of Jesus to Baruch is striking and poetic. Choose a paragraph or so of his dialogue and describe two or three things that he says.

   To expand the question, explain what makes it striking and poetic.

Discussion Questions

1. This play is called "The Bread of Heaven." Find sections about bread in the play. Jesus seems to be thinking of bread very differently than the crowds who ask Him for it. How is the bread Jesus is offering different from the kind of bread the crowds are looking for?

2. Baruch describes to Judas what he is hoping Jesus will do for the Zealots. He says there is no salvation for Israel unless

> when the moment comes, there's a popular rising, well timed, with an organisation and armed force behind it. That means *our* force and *our* organisation. The party is ready, as you know. All we need is a figurehead, a leader, a spell-binder to fire the imagination of the masses and make them fall in to march behind the party. . . . Brains aren't enough. You've got to appeal to the emotions—stir these peasants out of their slave mentality and give 'em something to fight and die for. (128)

How does this expectation contrast with what Jesus actually says and does in response to the crowd's wanting to make Him king?

3. In the notes, Sayers says of Judas: "In this play at last [Judas] defines himself. He has got the right idea, and holds it with passion and sincerity. But his intellectual pride, his jealousy, and a fundamental lack of generosity make him a ready ground for the sowing of seeds of suspicion" (123). Give one example from the play of Judas's pride or lack of generosity. How are pride and lack of generosity related to each other?

Life Questions—Journaling Assignment

Feel free to respond to the life questions here or to keep them in a separate journal used for meditative contemplation.

1. Describe one of your frailties—a weakness or a struggle or something that is hard for you. What would it be like to have Christ see it and understand it the way He did with the disciples?

2. Describe some of the best bread you've tasted, or several different kinds. Consider making bread for this lesson and thinking about what the lesson means in light of what bread is and Christ's comparison of Himself to it. What conclusions have you come to?

Write Your Own Discussion Questions

1.

2.

Play 6

The Feast of Tabernacles

Make Notes in Your Book

Tracing the Great Ideas

Great Ideas Quotes throughout the play for the theme *Forgiveness*

Forgiveness is the ability to recognize someone else's sin and to choose to extend a continued loving relationship to him. Sin functions a bit like debt—if you have sinned against someone, you owe it to him to try to heal the damage that you did. Fundamentally, though, we are not capable of healing the damage that we do to ourselves and the hurt we cause God, and so forgiveness is necessary if we are to have any sort of relationship.

Great Ideas Quotes throughout the play for the theme *The transcendent or numinous/The everyday*

Reading Questions

1. In the scene in which Caiaphas asks Judas to come and speak with the elders, Caiaphas makes this comment after Judas leaves: "That man has ideas. People with ideas are always jealous of their leaders. Yes, gentlemen, I think we may say we have now got Jesus of Nazareth where we want him" (162). How is Judas an "ideas man"?

   To expand this question: The comment by Caiaphas shows understanding of what aspect of human nature?

2. In this play, there is another reference to Roman mythology. A Roman character says that Jesus looks like a son of the immortals. Which character is it, and why might the comment be important in understanding that character's later actions in the play cycle?

Discussion Questions

1. In one part of the play, James and John ask if they should call down fire on the Samaritan village that has refused to host Jesus for the night. Jesus rebukes them and says that He has not come to destroy men's lives but to save them. James asks for forgiveness, and Jesus replies, "But have you forgiven these men? Forgiveness cannot help you if you cherish an unforgiving spirit" (153). What might this line mean? Other moments in which this subject arises include the parable of the unforgiving servant that follows it in the play, the conversation of the disciples after Jesus tells it, and later comments on forgiveness in the play.

2. The disciples describe the Transfiguration in terms that combine beauty and terror. With this in mind, reread the passage beginning with Peter saying, "We're all right here, if we talk quietly" and ending with John saying, "And even among those shadows there was peace" (154–156). Why and how do beauty and terror go together? (Hint: Check description of "the transcendent or numinous" theme.)

To expand this question: Have you had an experience that includes these elements?

3. How does Sayers end the conversation among James, John, and Peter about the Transfiguration? Why might she end there?

Life Questions—Journaling Assignment

Feel free to respond to the life questions here or to keep them in a separate journal used for meditative contemplation.

1. Think of the time when you were offered forgiveness and a time when you offered it to someone else. Are you conscious of a relationship between the two? When you are in a situation that asks you to forgive, do you consciously call up moments when you have been forgiven?

2. Have you had an experience that combines elements of beauty and terror?

Write Your Own Discussion Questions

1.

2.

Play 7

The Light and the Life

Make Notes in Your Book

Tracing the Great Ideas

Great Ideas Quotes throughout the play for the theme *Life/Death*

The contrast between life and death is one of the starkest in Scripture and in *The Man Born to Be King*. Beyond physical life and death, the contrast suggests also the difference between spiritual life and spiritual death. Spiritual life is found in a connection to God that allows the human being to flourish and to thrive in right relationship to the Creator of life. Spiritual death occurs when the human being is cut off from God. Because God is the center of all things, to be cut off from Him is to lose everything. If the state of being cut off from God continues, the human being will shrivel as certainly as a plant cut off from its roots.

Great Ideas Quotes throughout the play for the theme *Blindness/Sight*

Sight in *The Man Born to Be King* usually indicates the ability to see things spiritually, to understand the Kingdom of God. Blindness means the inability to see God's Kingdom.

Tell It Back

Reading Questions

1. What is the response Jesus gives to Lazarus's understanding of life?

   To expand this question: What does Jesus's response say about how Jesus wants Lazarus to understand the world?

2. When Jacob and Jesus first meet after Jacob has been excommunicated, Jacob is speaking to himself about the moon. What does he say?

   To expand this question: What does Jesus's response suggest about God's experience of His creation? For help, consult the notes for the actor playing Jesus as well.

3. Sayers is quite skillful about including short lines that say something very significant, often something the character delivering the lines is unaware of. Give an example.

To expand this question: Does the line you chose contain a hopeful irony that comments on Christ and His work? If so, what is it?

Discussion Questions

1. Look through the play and find references to Lazarus's attitude toward life. How would you describe it? How do these previous descriptions of Lazarus's relationship to life make his resurrection an especially meaningful moment in the play?

2. When the elders excommunicate Jacob, the man who has received his sight, they use this language: "Jacob ben-Issachar, pay heed, while I pronounce the sentence of excommunication. In the name of God, to whom be glory . . ." (179). How does the reading of that sentence show their spiritual blindness in the context of the play?

3. Revisit the conversation between Jacob and Jesus about seeing the moon for the first time (180), mentioned in the reading questions. Jacob says:

> Lord! what a lovely thing the moon is! To think I never seen it till last night. . . . Beg your pardon, sir—I didn't 'ear you comin'. . . . Now, that's queer. If I'd been blind, same as I used to be, I'd a-heard you right enough. Excuse me, but 'ave you ever looked at the moon? Really to *look* at it, I mean? You wouldn't think anything could be as pretty as that, if you wasn't 'ardened to it, in a manner of speaking. Think what you'd feel if it come all *fresh* to you, like it does to me—fresh as the day it was created.

Does this speech shed any light on why Jacob can see who Jesus is later in the conversation? How is his ability to see the moon connected to his ability to see the truth?

Life Questions—Journaling Assignment

Feel free to respond to the life questions here or to keep them in a separate journal used for meditative contemplation.

1. Do you identify with the wonder of characters such as Mary and Jacob? If not, do you wish you did? What has caused you wonder recently?

2. Take a look at the answer to reading question #3 in this play (in the TE):

For the mourner, the line is sorrowful at face value. For the audience, the line is ironic, showing that a reversal of death is coming. Rather than a tragic irony (one which emphasizes a sad contrast), this is a comic irony (which emphasizes a joyful reversal). Jesus is about to show that human life can be a comedy in the sense of a play with a joyful ending.

Have you ever considered life as a "comedy" and Christ as someone that has a sense of humor? Sayers has imagined it—how do you imagine Christ with a sense of humor? What might that look like?

Write Your Own Discussion Questions

1.

2.

Play 8
Royal Progress

Make Notes in Your Book

Tracing the Great Ideas

Great Ideas Quotes throughout the play for the theme *Wit/Humor (some of these might also double as quotes for the theme Life/Death)*

One thing Sayers consistently emphasizes in *The Man Born to Be King* is wit and humor, especially the wit and humor of Jesus. She reminds the audience frequently of how clever Jesus is and how much He enjoys laughter.

Great Ideas Quotes throughout the play for the theme *Pride/Humility*

Great Ideas Quotes throughout the play for the theme *The transcendent or numinous/The everyday*

Tell It Back

Reading Questions

1. Sayers says in the notes that this play is important to her plot structure (sequence of events within a piece of literature): "From the point of view of the plot-structure, this is the tie-up play which brings the Judas-Baruch story into close relation with the Caiaphas-Pilate situation" (193).

You may have noticed that Sayers quotes from *The Screwtape Letters* on page 198. This is one example of the many times that the Inklings and Sayers reference each other directly in their work.

Look at Baruch's letter to Jesus in scene 1, sequence 1. It forces a confrontation between Jesus and Judas in scene 1, sequence 3. How does it move the plot of the whole play cycle forward?

2. Caiaphas is clever and subtle at many levels. When he convinces Judas that Jesus should die, how does he make his case convincing to Judas?

3. We've talked already about Judas's pride and lack of generosity, and how the two are related. In this play, there is a huge contrast between the generosity of Mary and the coldness of Judas, who criticizes her for doing a very generous thing for Jesus. How is that contrast further heightened by the parable Jesus tells earlier in the scene?

Discussion Questions

1. In scene 1, sequence 2, one of the dinner guests notes that Jesus and Lazarus seem to be having a joke together (200). Later, when someone quizzes Lazarus on what it is like to be dead, Jesus laughs and says, "I'm sorry, Lazarus. You must do your best with it. But no State secrets." Why is the humor shared between Jesus and Lazarus an appropriate response to Lazarus's death and resurrection?

2. This is the play in which Judas's pride truly undoes him. Choose one moment of Sayers's notes on Judas or Judas's conversation with Caiaphas and discuss how pride drives Judas and why it is so dangerous.

3. In the notes for The Young Man (or the Rich Young Ruler), Sayers says:

> This Rich Young Ruler is one of those nice people who have always lived virtuously and gone to church, but have a perfectly well-founded feeling that that is not what the real saints and mystics understand by "religion". He has a hankering after some sort of a thing called "spiritual religion", which gives you lovely feelings. He would like to be at home in both worlds at once—to enjoy exalted religious emotions without disturbing his ordinary way of life. It is a shock to him to be told that real mystical experience is a catastrophic thing. (200)

Think of examples—from Scripture, history, or fiction—of moments when a person begins to understand the cost of encountering the transcendent.

Gimli in Lothlorien

Gimli, the Dwarf who joins the fellowship of the Ring, begins to recognize the cost of encountering the transcendent after the company visits Lothlorien. There he meets the Elven queen Galadriel, a lady who is fair and wise almost beyond understanding. Gimli is profoundly moved by her beauty and wisdom. When he leaves her kingdom, he says to one of the other characters:

> Tell me, Legolas, why did I come on this Quest? Little did I know where the chief peril lay! Truly Elrond spoke, saying that we could not foresee what we might meet upon our road. Torment in the dark was the danger that I feared, and it did not hold me back. But I would not have come, had I known the danger of light and joy. Now I have taken my worst wound in this parting, even if I were to go this night straight to the Dark Lord. Alas for Gimli son of Gloin! (470)

Life Questions—Journaling Assignment

Feel free to respond to the life questions here or to keep them in a separate journal used for meditative contemplation.

1. Think of a time when your faith demanded from you something difficult to give. Have you ever felt like the Rich Young Ruler, as the question above describes it: "to enjoy exalted religious emotions without disturbing his ordinary way of life"?

2. The lesson identifies Baruch and Judas as two people who use Jesus as a "tool" for the own ends. A milder form of this approach might be the idea that Christ is there to make our lives easier or better. How do you respond to this thought?

Write Your Own Discussion Questions

1.

2.

Play 9
The King's Supper

Make Notes in Your Book

Tracing the Great Ideas

Great Ideas Quotes throughout the play for the theme *Food/Feasting*

Great Ideas Quotes throughout the play for the theme *Pride/Humility*

Great Ideas Quotes throughout the play for the theme *Kingdom of God*

Tell It Back

Reading Questions

1. What does Jesus say about celebrating the Passover with His disciples?

   To expand this question: Have you ever thought about Christ yearning to feast with His people? Are there any aspects of your experience that help you understand how Christ longs to celebrate with us? Describe your own experiences of feasting as well as any sense you may have had that your presence and communion was desired by God.

2. Reread the poem "The Makers" at the very beginning of *The Man Born to Be King* (7–8). The poem looks forward to the fullness of God's Kingdom in a way that uses imagery drawn from the Last Supper, so it's helpful to look at it again in light of *The King's Supper*. Which stanzas especially interact with the Last Supper?

To expand this question: How do those stanzas imagine the full coming of God's Kingdom at the end of time?

3. Look at the language of Caiaphas when Judas has described how they can capture Jesus. Choose two words to describe the kind of language and tone he uses when speaking about a man's death.

To expand this question: Consider more broadly what this language suggests about Caiaphas and his attitude.

Discussion Questions

1. In this play, we see the moment when Christ begins the sacrament of communion. Sayers points out that the language He uses would have sounded shocking and even terrifying to His disciples. When Christ says, "Take and eat. This is my body which is broken for you," and "Drink, all of you, of this. For this is my blood of the new Covenant, which is poured out for many" (236), what are some of the reasons it would have been shocking? Feel free to refer to the play and the notes in your answer.

2. All along, Sayers has been emphasizing the difference between Peter and Judas. Peter is headstrong and impulsive, but humble. Judas has many good qualities, but is fundamentally proud. How is this difference evident in the way that each of them responds to Christ when He washes their feet?

3. Judging from their comments, what kind of Kingdom are the disciples expecting Jesus to usher in soon? How will the coming of the Kingdom contrast with their expectations?

Life Questions—Journaling Assignment

Feel free to respond to the life questions here or to keep them in a separate journal used for meditative contemplation.

1. Can you think of a time when you have behaved with unyielding determination as Judas did (either in actions or in thoughts and beliefs)? Explain.

2. Can you think of a time when you behaved with a complete, repentant turnaround as Peter did (either in actions or in thoughts and beliefs)? Explain.

Write Your Own Discussion Questions

1.

2.

Play 10
The Princes of This World

Make Notes in Your Book

Tracing the Great Ideas

Great Ideas Quotes throughout the play for the themes *Pride/Humility, Forgiveness, Freedom/Choice*

Individual choices and the freedom God gives to each person are huge themes in "The Triumph of Easter" and in *The Man Born to Be King*. Every human being has to choose whether to participate with God in the act of cultivating His creation or whether to rebel against Him and continue in sin. God can make something good from sinful human choices, but that in no way makes the sin itself good, and the person who continues to participate in sin will be destroyed by it. But God offers human beings a free choice—they can participate with Him or refuse to as they will. That choice is central for Sayers's understanding of human life and for the characters of *The Man Born to Be King*.

Great Ideas Quotes throughout the play for the themes *Kingship/Leadership, Kingdom of God*

Great Ideas Quotes throughout the play for the themes *God dying and rising in history, Christ as human and divine*

Reading Questions

1. In the notes on the play (247), Sayers discusses the difficulties of writing a scene for radio in which the main character "is required by the text to obtain his effects by 'keeping on saying nothing'" (247). She says that this works very well in a stage play, where an actor with good stage presence can hold the attention of the audience, but is much harder on the radio. She then lists her efforts to solve the problem. Choose one solution, state it, and explain if you think it is effective.

   To expand this question: How would you cope with the same problem as a scriptwriter?

2. In scene 1, sequence 3, why is it a helpful dramatic detail that Malchus is present when Peter denies Christ?

3. What is the final argument that the elders use to prevent Pilate from releasing Jesus? Why is it a clever argument to use?

Discussion Questions

1. This play shows the tragic end of Judas's story arc. Read Sayers's notes on Judas and Baruch's assessment of the situation (249–250), especially the section beginning, "In the first few minutes with Caiaphas" and ending, "pace, pace, pace and passion" (250). Consider this along with the section of the play in which Judas realizes what he has done and is caught in remorse (see his speech on 261, beginning, "There is no priest"). How is his response different from repentance? Do you find Sayers's interpretation of why Judas's sin is unforgivable convincing (see also notes, pp. 249–250)?

2. The opening play of the cycle, *Kings in Judaea*, offers several different models for human leadership and contrasts them all with the kingship of Christ. This play again offers a range of different models of earthly leadership. List two or more of the characters serving as models of leadership in *The Princes of This World*. How do they contrast with each other, and ultimately with Christ?

3. Sayers has already introduced the idea of Roman characters who meet Jesus and are reminded of Roman myths in which gods walk the earth disguised as men. How does she draw a contrast between the gods of Roman myth and the choices of Christ in the dialogue between Pilate and one of his assistants, Flavius (270)? Feel free to reference and quote sections from "The Greatest Drama Ever Staged," which deals with this theme.

Life Questions—Journaling Assignment

Feel free to respond to the life questions here or to keep them in a separate journal used for meditative contemplation.

1. How do you think and feel about the fact that Jesus cared about Malchus's ear at a time of great fear and chaos in His own life?

2. C.S. Lewis says that how we feel about a story is part of what the story is teaching us. How do you feel about the Christian story in light of this chapter and its discussion of other religious views, such as Roman mythology and its gods? To properly answer this question you should read the answer to discussion question #3 in the teacher's edition.

Write Your Own Discussion Questions

1.

2.

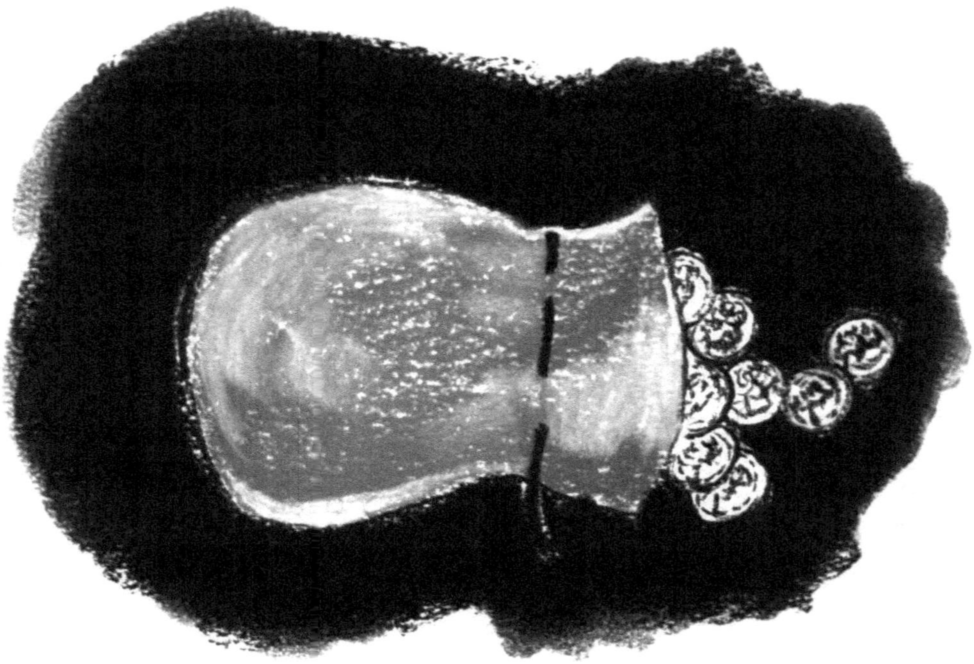

Play 11
King of Sorrows

Make Notes in Your Book

Tracing the Great Ideas

Great Ideas Quotes throughout the play for the themes *Blindness/Sight*, *Life/Death*

Great Ideas Quotes throughout the play for the theme *Redemption*

The theme of redemption, God's ability to make good things out of sinful human choices, is a strong one in Sayers's essays and in *The Man Born to Be King.*

Great Ideas Quotes throughout the play for the theme *God dying and rising in history*

Tell It Back

Reading Questions

1. Sayers imagines that Proclus and Balthazar meet again after all these years, with Proclus on duty at the cross and Balthazar again following the stars to seek Jesus. Why is this an important moment in the drama?

2. Dysmas (the name given by tradition to the repentant thief on the cross) speaks to Jesus after Jesus tells him, "Indeed and indeed I tell you—to-day you shall be with me in Paradise" (291). Even though he is confused, he grasps some essential knowledge about Christ through the haze. Choose one detail of what he says and describe how it shows his understanding of something true about Jesus.

3. Mary speaks to Balthazar after Christ is taken down from the cross. How does what she says recall her last meeting with Balthazar?

Discussion Questions

The first two questions will refer to the passage on page 279, in which the characters are headed to Golgotha to watch the crucifixion. Shadrach and one of the elders callously and sarcastically joke about it. One man, identified only as Elder, says it's a fine day, and Shadrach complains that it's too hot. Take a look at the dialogue between the Elder and Shadrach which begins at the start of scene 1 and ends with "what a comfort that is, to be sure!"

1. What is ironic about the Elder's asking, "You don't think there's any danger of that?" How does it reveal his spiritual blindness?

2. Shadrach ironically asks what would happen if Jesus said, "You can't kill me. I've broken the curse of Adam and banished death from the world" (279). Without realizing it, he is very close to the truth. But the scenario he proposes misses a key fact about the way Jesus actually breaks the curse of Adam. It is necessary for Christ to die in order to break the curse. Why is that necessary? Consider the following quotation from "The Triumph of Easter" as you formulate your answer.

> When Judas sinned, Jesus paid; He brought good out of evil, He led out triumph from the gates of Hell and brought all mankind out with Him; but the suffering of Jesus and the sin of Judas remain a reality. God did not abolish the fact of evil: He transformed it. He did not stop the Crucifixion: He rose from the dead. (*LDC*, 122)

3. How does Claudia's dream bring together the themes of Roman gods walking the earth and of Christ entering the world to die and rise in history?

Life Questions—Journaling Assignment

Feel free to respond to the life questions here or to keep them in a separate journal used for meditative contemplation.

1. Mary takes Jesus into her arms at the end of this play (297). Many have imagined what such a scene might look like, including Michelangelo, who made a sculpture of this moment. The sculpture, called *The Pietà*, is housed in St. Peter's Basilica in Rome. Find an image of it online and contemplate it, then write about what you saw. Feel free to write about it in poetry or prose.

2. Now read the Wikipedia entry on *The Pietà* and respond in writing again.

Write Your Own Discussion Questions

1.

2.

Play 12
The King Comes to His Own

Make Notes in Your Book

Tracing the Great Ideas

Great Ideas Quotes throughout the play for the theme *Pride/Humility*

Great Ideas Quotes throughout the play for the theme *Food/Feasting*

The theme of redemption, God's ability to make good things out of sinful human choices, is a strong one in Sayers's essays and in *The Man Born to Be King*.

Great Ideas Quotes throughout the play for the themes *God dying and rising in history, Christ as human and divine*

Tell It Back

Reading Questions

1. Sayers says in the notes (302), "This play contains a good deal about doors, and knockings at doors. It is, in fact, a play about the door between two worlds." Choose one moment in the play when a door is mentioned.

   To expand this question: Talk about how that moment might have bearing on understanding the door between two worlds.

2. When John and Mary Magdalene are talking about Judas, what is John afraid of?

To expand the question, describe Mary's answer and meditate on the following questions about its relation to your own life: Does Mary's description of what Jesus is like remind you of anything in your own experience? Have you ever had an experience of God's grace that was like this? Do you know any people who seem to cultivate this trait that Mary describes in Jesus—the ability to pursue goodness while understanding how much pain sin causes even to those who are sinning? Of course, the way that Jesus is able to do that will be different than the way that flawed human beings are able to do it, but describe as best you can how these people help you understand this quality Mary recognizes in Jesus.

3. Cleophas and his wife, Mary, describe how they met Jesus on the road to Emmaus. They recognized Jesus at the moment when He broke the bread for supper. Why do you think their recognition of Him occurred at that moment?

Discussion Questions

1. Even after John tells her that Peter cannot eat or sleep or forgive himself for betraying Christ, Mary Magdalene is confident that Peter's end will be different than that of Judas. What reason does she give for her hope? Why does she tell John to be bracing instead of soft with Peter?

2. Why do you think that one of the last things Jesus does on earth is to make breakfast for His disciples?

3. Sayers imagines what the disciples say as it becomes slowly more clear to them what it means for Jesus to be God as well as the Messiah. How does the following conversation (324) reflect what Sayers says in her essays about the nature of God becoming man in Christ? Pick one quotation from the context essays and talk about this section in light of it.

PETER *(who has suddenly become aware of some appalling implications):* Master—when I disowned you—when we disbelieved and doubted you—when we failed and deserted and betrayed you—is that what we do to God?

JESUS: Yes, Peter.

JAMES: Lord, when they mocked and insulted and spat upon you—when they flogged you—when they howled for your blood—when they nailed you to the cross and killed you—is that what we do to God?

JESUS: Yes, James.

JOHN: Beloved, when you patiently suffered all things, and went down to death with all our sins heaped upon you—is that what God does for us?

JESUS: Yes, John. For you, and with you, and in you, when you are freely mine. For you are not slaves, but sons. Free to be false or faithful, free to reject or confess me, free to crucify God or be crucified with Him, sharing the shame and sorrow, and the bitter cross and the glory. They that die with me rise with me also, being one with me, as I and my Father are one.

Life Questions—Journaling Assignment

Feel free to respond to the life questions here or to keep them in a separate journal used for meditative contemplation. In reading question #2 for this lesson, there are a series of questions you are invited to answer as part of an expanded version of the question. Take some time to contemplate whichever part of the expanded questions you would like to pursue further as a life question.

1. Does Mary's description of what Jesus is like remind you of anything in your own experience? Have you ever had an experience of God's grace that was like this?

Here Sayers talks about the door between two worlds, the door between heaven and earth. C.S. Lewis is also interested in doors between worlds. The most famous example is probably the wardrobe through which the Pevensie children first enter Narnia, but all the Narnia books are alive with the possibility of links among worlds. The Wood Between the Worlds in *The Magician's Nephew* is another example of this idea. One of the reasons Lewis uses this idea so much is his belief (shared with Sayers) in a spiritual world that interacts with our own world even though it is unseen.

2. Do you know any people who seem to cultivate this trait that Mary describes in Jesus, the ability to pursue goodness while understanding how much pain sin causes even to those who are sinning? Of course, the way that Jesus is able to do that will be different than the way that a flawed human being is able to do it, but do you know anyone who helps you understand what Mary means here?

Write Your Own Discussion Questions

1.

2.

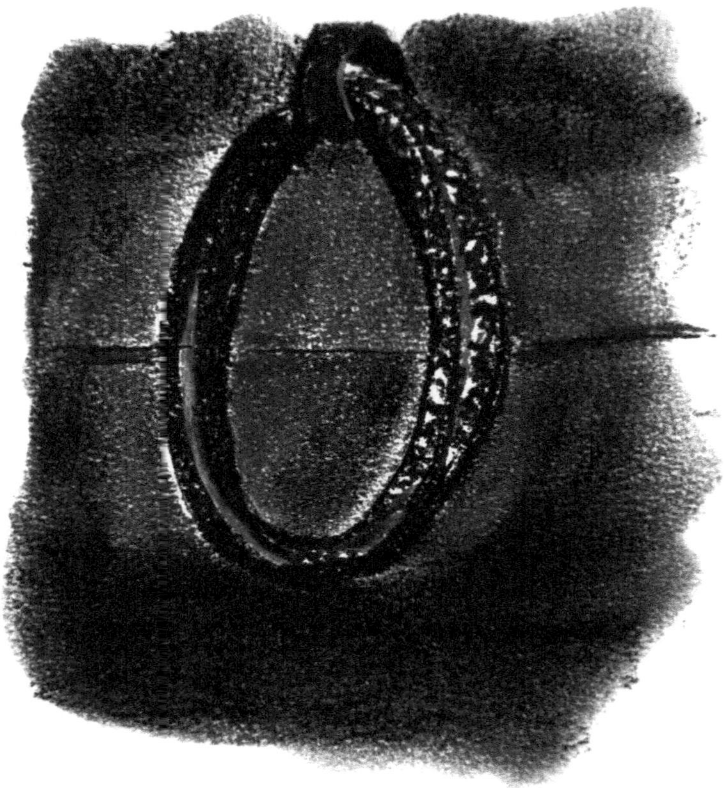

Quotation Identification

We have chosen memorable quotations from each play that are significant to *The Man Born to Be King* and that guide you through the great ideas you have studied. Identify who said each quote and give a sentence or two that describes the context of the quote within the moment of the story.

Play 1: *Kings in Judaea*

"You cannot rule men by love."

Play 2: *The King's Herald*

"We're crossing Jordan, just like Joshua and the Ark."

Play 3: *A Certain Nobleman*

" 'Too late'—I am eighty years old, and I thought 'too late'—too late now to behold the Kingdom—but the Bridegroom came at midnight."

Play 4: *The Heirs to the Kingdom*

"And he smiled—you know the way he smiles sometimes all of a sudden—and he says, 'Follow me'. I couldn't believe my ears I tumbled out of my desk, and away he went up the street, and I went after him. I could hear people laughing—and somebody spat at me—but I didn't seem to care."

Play 5: *The Bread of Heaven*

"If only you could hear his voice as we heard it then, speaking about happiness, and the blessed Kingdom of God. I hear it now . . . it will be in my ears till I die . . ."

Play 6: *The Feast of Tabernacles*

"Madam, it is the feast of water and of light, when we give God thanks for the harvest—for the good rain that swells the corn and the blessed sun that ripens it."

Play 7: *The Light and the Life*

"Think what you'd feel if it come all *fresh* to you, like it does to me—fresh as the day it was created."

Play 8: *Royal Progress*

"Give me a sign, for now is the moment to strike and seize your kingdom."

Play 9: *The King's Supper*

"I have set my hand to the plough. Through mud or blood, the feet must follow."

Play 10: *The Princes of This World*

"I tell you, Flavius, I've never had much use for religion. But those old stories. . . . They say the gods have walked the earth before now—"

Play 11: *King of Sorrows*

"I have found him as my dream foretold, by the tall tree on the hill."

Play 12: *The King Comes to His Own*

"The Master's the only good man I ever met who knew how miserable it felt to be bad. It was as if he got right inside you, and *felt* all the horrible things you were doing to yourself."

Here are some activities that may enhance your experience of these plays. Most students remember and learn material with which they have the opportunity to engage and which they enjoy. These remind the students that academic work is related to the lives they are living and to pleasure. The activities give students another mode in which to contemplate the material. Feel free to invent your own enrichment activities as well.

Reader's Theater/Acting

Choose a play from the cycle, or several scenes. Choose people to read each part and then give a reading (or if you're feeling really ambitious, memorize your parts). This can be done informally in a classroom setting, or can be organized as an event with guest participants and/or an audience. If it is a formal event, we recommend doing the casting and practice ahead of time.

Memorization

1. Many of the characters have very striking monologues at one point or another. Choose a monologue from the play to memorize. Or work with a friend or two and memorize a section of dialogue.
2. Memorize a strong paragraph from one of Sayers's essays, the notes, or the introductory poem "The Makers." It might be fun to recite this to a friend, or if a whole class is memorizing, to give a performance.

Music

1. Sayers discusses the music used in the play cycle at the end of the introduction (28). Do some research and see if you can find any of the music she mentions, and listen to it.
2. Consider composing your own tunes for one of the following:
   a. The hymn in play 5 (137, "All they that to the sea go down")
   b. The soldiers' song in play 10 (269, "Bring me garlands")
   c. Mary Magdalene's song in play 11 (290, "Soldier, soldier, why will you roam?")

Recording

Choose one play or a section of a play and make your own recording of it. Choose actors, plan sound effects, and decide if it needs any music. Then record it.

Visual Art

Pick a scene or character (or a different character if you have already done so in a Tell It Back exercise) and illustrate it in a sketch or some other medium (including 3D). Or make a verbal collage around a significant image from the story that brings together important and lasting words that you encountered in the play.

Gathering Your Thoughts for the Final Essay

As you come to the end of the play cycle, you may wish to spend some time pondering questions about the work as a whole. Here are a few ideas.

1. What did you most enjoy about the play cycle, as you review the whole thing?
2. Revisit the list of great ideas themes found below (pp. 141–142). Which theme was most striking to you? Why did it stand out? Please note that all of your discussion questions were based on these themes, so revisiting your answers or the questions themselves may help you to best answer this question. Choose one to three themes, and collect all the quotes book-wide (go back through your great ideas theme quotes) related to those themes.

   Try to describe how your knowledge of the theme(s) you chose has been changed and deepened by the experience of reading and discussing *The Man Born to Be King*.
3. Sometimes a book or a discussion gives us questions to consider for a long time afterward—perhaps weeks, months, or even years. It's hard to tell sometimes when you've found one, but some books even raise questions you may be asking for the rest of your life. What are some questions you will take with you after reading *The Man Born to Be King*? Throughout the guide you have been creating your own discussion questions. Create one to three of them for the work as a whole now that you have encountered the entire play cycle.

Final Essay Goals

As you wrap up your study of *The Man Born to Be King*, you will write a final essay. This essay is an opportunity to put together much of what you have learned about a particular theme or topic across the whole course of the play cycle. This essay has several purposes:

1. To put into one place passages that are particularly important in your understanding of a theme, so that you can see what the play cycle is saying about them as a whole
2. To consider how your understanding of a theme or topic has changed or deepened over the course of the time spent with these plays
3. To sum up your understanding of the theme or topic so that you can revisit it later and remember what you learned through reading the play cycle
4. To provide a springboard for further questions and thought about the theme or topic over time. Ideally, a paper serves not only as a summing up of what you have learned, but as a source of ideas about what you might learn in the future as well. A paper should be something complete in the sense of a well-worked out explanation of what you have learned. But the paper doesn't begin as complete; it begins with a thought that leads to a thesis (argument) and often changes as you write it. As you write, be alert for ideas you might write about in the future, and for questions you may want to ask yourself over time in your life as well as in your formal education.

Final Essay Topics

Now that you are nearing completion of this study, you will make an argument presenting Sayers's demonstration of a great idea in the life of a character and the plot surrounding that character. Look at the sample topic questions that we pose below. You may choose one of the ones we have spelled out, or you may create your own using the great idea, character(s), and circumstance(s) of your choice (see the great idea themes listed after our sample questions). Your essay should include textual support (remember to look at the quotes you collected for each great idea), and you should also consider relevant excerpts from Sayers's context essays. In one to six pages (or whatever length your teacher requires), you should defend your thesis in an argumentative essay format (make an argument and support it with details and description as well as quotation and examples). You might wish to take a look at the teacher's edition for sample papers on the themes of Restoration, Forgiveness, and God dying and rising in history; there is also a lively summary and illustration of the ideas in Sayers's essay "The Greatest Drama Ever Staged."

Our main goal here is to help you begin making connections and forming arguments about ideas that run throughout a book. You have sorted the pieces of the puzzle into piles of similar colors (by reading, marking the book, taking notes, answering questions, and having discussions); now you can put the puzzle together (the difference being a puzzle has one way to go together, but themes can be discussed and argued in endless ways). Choose a question from the suggestions below that has particular significance in your own life—perhaps one that you have struggled with or has been particularly challenging in your own life or the life of your family. This will make your writing stronger and more purposeful. Keep in mind that there are numberless ways to complete this assignment. The following elements will help to guide you regardless of the thesis that you choose.

- Support your thesis with the great ideas quotations you recorded.
- Support your thesis with the essays you read alongside this book.
- Develop your ideas with examples.
- Help us to see with description how your examples prove your argument.
- Explain your quotations and how they fit your argument.
- Consider what argument someone might make against yours and address those concerns as part of your defense.
- Conclude by restating your thesis with the depth of understanding you have established in the course of the writing.

Sample Topic Questions

1. One of the major themes explored in the plays and in this literature guide is the contrast between pride and humility. Judas is the major figure who most shows what pride is like in *The Man Born to Be King*. Now that you have read the whole play cycle, choose a more humble character and write an essay contrasting that character and Judas. Show how that person's responses to Jesus over the course of the play cycle illustrate the contrast between pride and humility. Choices might include (but are not limited to): Judas and Peter, Judas and John, Judas and Matthew, Judas and Mary Magdalene.
2. In one way or another, most of the leaders in *The Man Born to Be King* are answering the question, "What does it mean to be a king?" Write an essay contrasting two different approaches to earthly leadership shown by characters in the play cycle. It might be especially fruitful to contrast one or all of the Wise Men, whose approach to earthly kingship is wise if imperfect, with one of the other leaders who is less wise. However, it might also be interesting to compare characters such as Caiaphas and Pontius Pilate, who both make terrible choices in the course of the play cycle but who do have very different approaches to leadership.
3. What have you learned about the Kingdom of God? You might pick one image or anecdote Jesus uses to describe it and think about all the things it could mean, or explore several images or anecdotes and how they complement each other and fill out your understanding of the Kingdom. Or you might describe the process of what you learned about the Kingdom over the course of reading the plays. Has your understanding of it changed?

4. Choose one of the other great ideas (or one you have taken notes about on your own) and write an essay discussing how your understanding of it has deepened as you have thought about it over the course of reading all the plays. Give quotations from Sayers that are particularly meaningful to you and demonstrate what you learned about the theme from them.

As we have done in earlier questions for this section, choose a character or characters, or circumstances, and argue for the relationship between them and the great idea. To help you prepare, go back to read the places in the guide that focused on that theme, and take a look at the quotes you have gathered over the course of the twelve plays. We have bolded the part of the great idea definition in the list below that might be especially useful to you in developing a thesis.

Great Ideas Themes in *The Man Born to Be King*

Kingship/Leadership: As might be guessed from the title, this play cycle spends a great deal of time exploring the nature of kingship and leadership. It keeps returning to the question of what it looks like to guide or rule people well, especially for someone who holds a political office. **It presents several different models not only of how people should rule, but also of how people do rule—that is, *The Man Born to Be King* tries to present a realistic picture of how leadership often works, as well as a model of how it should work.**

Kingdom of God: Sayers spends a good deal of time in *The Man Born to Be King* presenting models of how earthly leadership does work and sometimes of how it should work. But more importantly, the play cycle constantly affirms that there is a different and better kind of kingdom, the Kingdom of God. The Kingdom Jesus is leading looks very different from the kingdoms of this world. Sayers draws on the biblical language of the Kingdom of God to flesh out this distinction in the course of the play cycle. In Scripture, Christ is always using metaphor, story, and analogy to describe the nature of the life and world He desires human beings to participate in with Him. **He describes this life and world as the Kingdom of God, and uses all sorts of descriptions of it that invite thought and work to understand—it is like a mustard seed, it is like a king having a feast, it is like a merchant buying a beautiful pearl, and so on. Sayers works with this scriptural language to create a sense of God's Kingdom as something centrally important in the play cycle.**

Prophecy: Prophecy is the prediction of future events. In *The Man Born to Be King* it is an important theme, because God's prophets predicted the coming of the Messiah and many of the things Christ and those around Him would do. Prophecy also ties to the ideas about individual choice and freedom discussed in the essay "The Triumph of Easter." Predictions made by God's true prophets will come true either way, but the individual has a choice about how to participate in them. An individual can freely participate in God's will and have the prophecies come true in a good way in the self; or an individual can fight against God and have the prophecies come true upon the self in a destructive way. **The individual has the free choice of how to interact with God and with what He says about the future.**

God dying and rising in history: This theme recurs in Sayers's essays, that **in Christ all the myths of dying and rising gods come true in the concrete facts of history.**

Pride/Humility: **The contrast between pride and humility is one of the most central themes of *The Man Born to Be King*. Pride is the sin that makes someone turn inward toward the self, that makes a person unable to desire things outside the self rightly, even God. Humility is the virtue that allows the self to see its right place in the world, to enjoy belonging to a world wider and greater than the self, and ultimately to enjoy and worship God.**

Food/Feasting: **Food and feasting is a central metaphor in Scripture, and Sayers frequently uses it in *The Man Born to Be King*. The imagery of food often suggests God's desire to nurture and provide for His people, and feasting brings to mind His longing to celebrate with them. Feasting also often suggests the end of time, when God will renew all things and make a feast for His people.**

Christ as human and divine: **Sayers emphasizes the importance of Christ's being both God and man over and over in her essays and in the plays themselves. It is the fact that Jesus is both man and God that lets Him bring redemption—if He were only God, He could not suffer human troubles and through that understand humanity and pay the price for our sins. If He were only man, He could not bring about transformation in the human condition.**

The transcendent or numinous/The everyday: Throughout *The Man Born to Be King*, there are moments when human beings confront something vastly beyond themselves and are moved, changed, or often completely undone by that thing. They see its beauty and are overpowered by it. This mode of experience often comes from a confrontation with something that is transcendent, such as an angel, or more often in *The Man Born to Be King* from a direct confrontation with the glory of God, the source of transcendence. This kind of astonishing and catastrophic experience of the spiritual world can be described by the adjective "numinous," which comes from a word meaning "spirit" or "god." While other religions and many mythologies have a concept of the numinous or transcendent, in Christian thought this kind of experience stems ultimately from God's glory. There are many moments in the play cycle when someone tries to describe this kind of mysterious and awe-inspiring experience; pay attention to that character as you read. **While the experience of the transcendent or the numinous sometimes seems entirely removed from everyday life, the two are often closer than you would think in *The Man Born to Be King*. Watch for moments when the two appear together and think about what Sayers might be saying about their relationship.**

Forgiveness: Forgiveness is the ability to recognize someone else's sin and choose to extend a continued loving relationship to him. Sin functions a bit like debt—if you have sinned against someone, you owe it to him to try to heal the damage that you did. **Fundamentally, though, we are not capable of healing the damage that we do to ourselves and the hurt we cause God, and so forgiveness is necessary if we are to have any sort of relationship.**

Life/Death: The contrast between life and death is one of the starkest in Scripture and in *The Man Born to Be King*. **Beyond physical life and death, the contrast suggests also the difference between spiritual life and spiritual death. Spiritual life is found in a connection to God that allows the human being to flourish and to thrive in right relationship to the Creator of life. Spiritual death occurs when the human being is cut off from God.** Because God is the center of all things, to be cut off from Him is to lose everything. If the state of being cut off from God continues, the human being will shrivel as certainly as a plant cut off from its roots.

Blindness/Sight: **Sight in *The Man Born to Be King* usually indicates the ability to see things spiritually, to understand the Kingdom of God. Blindness means the inability to see God's Kingdom.**

Wit/Humor: One thing Sayers consistently emphasizes in *The Man Born to Be King* is wit and humor, especially the wit and humor of Jesus. **She reminds the audience frequently of how clever Jesus is and how much He enjoys laughter.**

Freedom/Choice: Individual choices and the freedom God gives to each person are huge themes in "The Triumph of Easter" and in *The Man Born to Be King*. Every human being has to choose whether to participate with God in the act of cultivating His creation or whether to rebel against Him and continue in sin. God can make something good from sinful human choices, but that in no way makes the sin itself good, and the person who continues to participate in sin will be destroyed by it. **But God offers human beings a free choice—they can participate with Him or refuse to as they will. That choice is central for Sayers's understanding of human life and for the characters of *The Man Born to Be King*.**

Redemption: **The theme of redemption, God's ability to make good things out of sinful human choices, is a strong one in Sayers's essays and in *The Man Born to Be King*.**

We are including four sample papers on some of the great ideas themes traced through this guide. The first two were written by college students and in both cases are excerpts from larger papers. The third is an example of how sample question #4 (see p. 146) might be answered in an essay. In addition, there is a reflection paper that contains the summary of an essay and a personal response that requires student engagement and consideration but is not as polished and argument driven as the others.

Sample Paper 1

Restoration in *The Man Born to Be King*

In the writings of the Inklings, the theme of biblical restoration is found in the lives of several characters. Restoration is defined by Merriam-Webster as something being brought back to a former condition. In 1 John 1:9 we read that "if we confess our sins, He [God] is faithful and righteous to forgive us our sins and to cleanse us from all unrighteousness" (NASB). This verse speaks of being returned to the condition we were in before we sinned. The verse before this one speaks of the self-deception that occurs when individuals think they have done nothing wrong.

The characters I will focus on experience a falling away or breaking faith with God. They have chosen paths that are not part of God's best plan for their lives, and their reactions, once they come to this realization, are starkly different. The gaps between these characters' responses are as vast as their ability to trust God to cross the gap and bring them back to Himself. In these next pages, we will look at the characters of Edmund in *The Lion, the Witch and the Wardrobe* and Simon Peter from *The Man Born to Be King*, and how their lives are restored. We will also look at Gollum from *The Fellowship of the Ring* and Judas Iscariot in *The Man Born to Be King* to see why they reject restoration.

. . .

[We have excerpted the section of the paper that relates directly to *The Man Born to Be King*]

. . .

Another character who finds himself in a similar predicament is Simon Peter from *The Man Born to Be King*. He has many faults, yet they do not condemn him to a life of misery. In the beginning, Sayers describes Simon Peter as impulsive and self-confident, characteristics that lead him to many hardships before he learns humility (55). Unlike Edmund, Simon Peter goes back and forth between doing right and doing wrong. Sometimes he has moments of intense breakthrough when he sees the truth, and other times he blindly stumbles into pits of failure.

Simon Peter can be very harsh; for instance, in the fourth play, he gets upset with Philip for being swindled out of their hard-earned money. On the other hand, he displays humility when he gets the water to wash Judas's feet (105) and later, struggles when Jesus comes to wash his own feet (232). Later, through witnessing the miraculous large catch of fish, Simon Peter realizes Jesus's divinity and his own sinfulness (106–107). He is usually quick to protect and defend Jesus, but sometimes in doing so he misses Jesus's main point, such as the call to love our enemies, particularly the Romans (115).

He is a simple man with a raw quality before God. Jesus reassures him through a parable that even though he grumbles, his good heart will lead him to right actions in the end. As he falls more in love with Jesus, we see how he follows true to Christ and he will eventually do great things for the Kingdom of God. His great enthusiasm is shown in his response to Jesus's appearance walking on the water, but also his weakness when he looks to himself and falls (137). Later, as Jesus asks the disciples who they think He is,

Simon, through inspiration, affirms Jesus's identity as the Son of the Living God. In response, Jesus renames him Peter and prophesies that he whose faith has been like shifting sand will become the Rock that the Church is built upon. Then, immediately following this affirmation, Peter, who does not understand Jesus's self-prophecy of suffering, speaks out against it and is rebuked. Once again he feels like a failure and is confused (140).

One of Peter's keys to success is his realization of his wrongs and his repentance. A big step in restoration is admitting failure and looking to God to make it right. Peter receives redemption and restoration through Jesus's actions. Not only is he restored but he is also lifted up to a place of honor. This is much like Edmund's character being raised to kingship and identified as the Just in the last chapter of *The Lion, the Witch and the Wardrobe.*

. . .

[We have excerpted the section of the paper that relates directly to *The Man Born to Be King*]

. . .

In the story, Judas has a better understanding of Jesus's parables than the other disciples do. There are many occasions when the other disciples speak of Judas's cleverness and ability to see ahead. Upon joining Jesus, Philip quickly hands over the ministry's finances to Judas because of his "head for figures" (108). Prompted by his passionate ideals, Judas blindly stumbles into corruption and danger. Judas disagrees with Baruch's method of bringing justice through a political revolution. Yet, in the end, his ideals lead him to make the wrong assumptions of Jesus. Judas even boldly declares that he would kill Jesus with his own hands if he were to "let down" his idea of him (130). He later confesses that he is not afraid of dying but rather of not being right about Jesus being incorruptible (184, 260–261).

Sayers reassures the reader of Judas's sincerity. He is well liked among the disciples, but at the same time, he is jealous of Jesus's affection for them and judges them as fools when they do not "understand" Jesus as he does. Sayers describes Judas's pride, growing jealousy, and lack of generosity as seeds for suspicion of Jesus's motives. The story turns tragically as his suspicion grows. He is lacking trust, and there are several occasions when Jesus confronts him, and Judas chooses to lie instead of confess his doubts. He even attempts to encourage the other disciples to suspect Jesus of possible corruption (184). In the scene with Mary Magdalene, Jesus confronts Judas for being unkind to Mary and hopes to redeem him by bringing his mistreatment into the light. Just as Jesus graciously offers redemption to Judas, God pursues humanity to bring it unto restoration. This is witnessed in the lives of Edmund, Peter, Gollum, and Judas.

Judas's understanding decreases as his doubts take root. He questions Jesus because he wants to understand what is going on in order to exert control (204–205). As soon as he hears Jesus speaking of Jerusalem's destruction, he assumes Jesus is referring to armies rising up to revolt. Sayers's interpretation of Jesus's last attempt to rescue Judas from himself shows Jesus's awareness of Judas's betrayal (233). In the end, Judas is finally consumed by despair due to his lack of humility and generosity. Once again, Judas is embittered by his desire to be in control (261). He is repulsed by Jesus's innocence. He cannot bear that Jesus is the better man. He feels locked into his plan to "fix" things, but even then doubts his harsh judgment. In the end, Judas realizes he is guilty of betraying an innocent man and is left with only his self-loathing. He is ashamed of his actions; however, his pride hinders him from seeking Jesus's forgiveness. He meets a tragic end, but, like Gollum, if it were not for his selfish actions, others would not be saved! This shows how God is able to use all situations to redeem those who will accept His gift.

. . .

[We have excerpted the section of the paper that relates directly to
The Man Born to Be King: conclusion of the paper]

. . .

Ironic events show how evil finds evil: Edmund is found by the wicked White Witch and Judas is caught doing the very thing he rebukes Baruch for suggesting. In all these characters the need for restoration is overwhelmingly evident. In Edmund's and Peter's lives, their flaws do not withhold them from humility and the ability to change. On the other hand, Gollum and Judas choose to not confess their shortcomings and because of this remain bound to sin. This shows the need to accept God's restoration. It is already available and God earnestly seeks us out, but He leaves it in the hands of the individual. Unlike Gollum, who holds on to what is most precious to him, Mary Magdalene gives her most precious possession in an act of worship. She does not take it lightly that her sins are forgiven, but she humbly receives the gift. In Edmund and Peter this newfound freedom encourages bold, loving actions.

Sample Paper 2

Below is an excerpt from a larger paper in which a student takes on the subject of forgiveness in *The Man Born to Be King* and writes about its nature using the thesis statement that is highlighted in bold below (in two sentences—one at the start of the paragraph and one at the end).

Forgiveness in *The Man Born to Be King*

Sayers's *The Man Born to Be King* provides several examples of how Jesus, the paragon of virtue, forgives those who transgress against Him. After Thomas exclaims, "You are my Lord and my God" when he finally sees Jesus, there is an important stage direction that follows: "The crucial word is spoken at last, and received in complete silence" (324). Though Jesus goes on to say, "Thomas, because you have seen me, you have believed. Blessed are they that have not seen and yet have believed" (324), that moment of silence seems to suggest that forgiveness, or perhaps more accurately, reconciliation takes place between Jesus and Thomas in that pregnant pause. In a sense forgiveness is implied (though sinful actions and doubt are not excused). Thomas's words are "received in silence." This is such an important detail. It's as if Thomas exclaims that he no longer doubts, asks for forgiveness, receives/accepts forgiveness, and thus reconciliation is born all in one moment. Accepting forgiveness is crucial to reconciliation (thus the two-person effort as opposed to the individual effort of forgiving). **Forgiveness has to be offered and then accepted in order for reconciliation to have a foundation.**

Peter, James, and John all ask Jesus questions regarding sin and forgiveness toward the very end of the play, and it is important to explore these questions and answers to perceive how Sayers demonstrates forgiveness through this dialogue. Let's begin with Peter's question: "Master—when I disowned you—when we disbelieved and doubted you—when we failed and deserted and betrayed you—is that what we do to God?" (324). Here we see some of the transgressions that have been made against Jesus. Anyone who has been doubted, let down, deserted, betrayed, or disowned understands how incredibly painful it is and how difficult it would be to forgive anyone who has done any of those things (let alone all of them). Yet we will soon see in Jesus's response to John that He offers forgiveness to all sinners no matter the sins they have committed.

Very similar to Peter's questions, James asks Jesus, "Lord, when they mocked and insulted and spat upon you—when they flogged you—when they howled for your blood—when they nailed you to the cross and killed you—is that what we do to God?" (324). Anyone who has the misfortune of understanding what it's like to be hated, insulted, mocked, or spat upon would understand how incredibly hard it is to forgive the people who hate and insult and spit. Yet when Jesus responds to John, we see that Jesus does forgive.

Now finally John takes the conversation in a new direction when he asks, "Beloved, when you patiently suffered all things, and went down to death with all our sins heaped upon you—is that what God does for us?" (324). The focus is now shifted from what humankind does to God to what God does for humankind. Jesus responds:

> Yes, John. For you, and with you, and in you, when you are freely mine. For you are not slaves, but sons. Free to be false or faithful, free to reject or confess me, free to crucify God or be crucified with Him, sharing the shame and sorrow, and the bitter cross and the glory. They that die with me rise with me also, being one with me, as I and my Father are one. (324)

Jesus's response is packed with information about forgiveness. One of the most important things is the freedom we have, which includes the freedom to choose to accept forgiveness or deny it. Since we are not slaves, we do not have to forgive or accept forgiveness. But if we do not offer forgiveness, how can we expect to be forgiven? And if we do not accept forgiveness, there will never be reconciliation. Jesus forgives Peter despite his transgressions; he forgives James; he forgives all those who harmed him or mocked him; he forgives John; he even offers forgiveness to the traitor Judas—he offers forgiveness to us all. We can be like Judas and doubt the power of that forgiveness or we can choose to accept it.

Jesus's forgiveness is obviously not feigned. He instantaneously offers forgiveness to everyone for sins that would take most people years to forgive if they ever forgave at all. We see Jesus's heart through His dialogue with these characters. Note that Jesus does not condone their actions, just as He does not condone Thomas's doubt, but in His heart He forgives them and they accept that forgiveness. Notice the distinction between forgiveness and excusing/condoning and the distinction between forgiveness and reconciliation.

Sample Paper 3

God Dying and Rising in History in *The Man Born to Be King*

In writing *The Man Born to Be King*, Dorothy Sayers brings to life the story of Jesus Christ. In this well-known Christian doctrine, God sends His Son, Jesus, to the world as a human being; Jesus dies on the cross to save humanity from sin; and then He defeats death by rising from the dead. There are other myths that tell similar tales, but the story of Jesus has a very important, unique factor that makes it astonishing: *it is true*. In this series of plays Dorothy Sayers emphasizes the incarnation as what distinguishes the Christian myth, showing us that because the death of Jesus Christ happened in history, the "dying god" myth turns into truth.

In terms of mythology, Jesus Christ is not the only god who died and was resurrected (12). Sayers reminds us in "The Greatest Drama Ever Staged" that, for example, "The Egyptian Osiris died and rose again[, and] Æschylus in his play, *The Eumenides*, reconciled man to God by the theory of a suffering Zeus" (*LDC*, 3). As a result, the culture that Jesus lived in would have been familiar with the concept of a dying god. It is important to note, though, that "in most theologies, the god is supposed to have suffered and died in some remote and mythical period of prehistory" (*LDC*, 3). In *The Man Born to Be King*, the Roman centurion Proclus describes Jesus to a fellow soldier: "He's a carpenter's son from Nazareth, and they say he's a miracle-worker. . . . A good man, I thought, with something godlike in his face. When Apollo the All-Healer took human shape, He might have looked like that" (110). In other words, Proclus recognizes something divine in Jesus. He does not, however, consider the possibility that Jesus *is* divine, because incarnations like that of Apollo did not take place in humanity's time frame. Jesus, however, was actually born into human history.

While the society Jesus entered did not expect Him to be a god incarnate, they would have been familiar with the historical presence of religious figures or messengers of the divine. Sayers explains, "Plenty of founders of religions have had dates, and some of them have been prophets or avatars of the Divine" (12). Consequently, society understood Jesus as a prophet or a teacher, but that He might actually be a god Himself was out of the question. In *The Man Born to be King*, a Galilean woman named Rebecca expresses concern to Jesus's mother regarding Jesus's ministry. She comments, "I think I ought to warn you that people are beginning to say rather dangerous things. Suggesting that Jesus might be the Messiah and all that—quite ridiculous, of course, to people who know him, but it's really not *safe* these days, and if you could just drop him a hint—" (82). Rebecca is comfortable with the idea that Jesus is a "prophet or preacher or something" (82), but she recognizes that Jesus's claims to be divine are so out of the ordinary that they are actually dangerous.

The combination of Jesus's divinity and His presence in human history makes Him "unique among gods and men" (12). If Jesus were singularly divine, He would have been like all other gods, and "His immortality [would] mean nothing to us" (*LDC*, 5). In other words, the resurrection of a god is not significant. But He was not only divine; He was also human, and therefore His life is a fact of human history. On the other hand, if Christ were merely human, Sayers explains, "His death [would be] no more important than yours or mine" (*LDC*, 5). But "the man we hanged was God Almighty" (*LDC*, 4)—that is, He died in history as both god and human. Through the incarnation, He takes the dying god myth and establishes it as a historical fact.

That the myth of Jesus Christ is true—that is, that it really took place—is astonishing. Sayers helps us understand the significance of the *fact* of Jesus Christ by emphasizing His place in history in Claudia's dream. In the dream, Claudia asks the captain of the ship how God could die, and he responds, " 'Don't you remember? They crucified him. He suffered under Pontius Pilate' " (295). The captain's response solidifies for us that Jesus's death has become a historical fact. In her notes on this section of the play, Sayers explains that the captain responds to Claudia "as one would remind a child of a forgotten lesson" (278), as if to say, "Oh, but you know that. Everybody knows it" (278). Jesus's death is a well-remembered event of history.

Because it is a fact widely known, however, sometimes we forget how surprising and significant it is that Jesus was both myth and fact. Sayers explains, the story of Jesus Christ "is summarised quite clearly in the creeds of the Church, and if we think it dull it is because we either have never really read those amazing documents or have recited them so often and so mechanically as to have lost all sense of their meaning" (*LDC*, 1). Sayers's plays help awaken our imagination to the awe that Jesus's story merits. Through her vivid depiction, we recognize that Jesus actually lived, unlike any other god. He alone entered our history, and in doing so He actualized the myth of the dying god.

Sample Paper 4

Reflection and Summary on
"The Greatest Drama Ever Staged" by Sayers

In both "The Greatest Drama Ever Staged" as well as "The Dogma Is the Drama," Sayers says that Jesus has been watered down and made meek and mild and a subject of tedium. She asserts how misguided an assumption that is, that Jesus is far too dynamic and dangerous a character to be relegated to the yawns of drowsy summertime Sunday mornings. Sayers in *The Man Born to Be King* is not creating a new Jesus that we are allowed to be interested in; she is reminding us that Jesus Christ is in fact the most radical mover that our history has seen, and that even those alive at the time were aware of His significance (which seems rare these days. I watched MSNBC report that Justin Bieber now has a girlfriend and I just wanted to smack my forehead). When we were asked to examine some example of dogma in light of Sayers's thesis, and to find occurrences of her dramatizing in the play, all I could think was that in the very person of Jesus we have installed a dogma that requires the revitalizing that *The Man Born to Be King* provides.

I was reading about French idioms the other day, and found one humorous one that is used to describe good food or wine. The saying literally goes, "This goes down like a little Jesus in velvet trousers!" Which still amuses me even as I type this, but I see in regards to dogma something disturbing here. It's as though the author of this idiom sat for a moment in order to think of the softest or least offensive thing he could find and landed on Jesus. Why? Jesus seems to be this Play-Doh that people are tempted to fashion and press into certain roles for various purposes. Jesus the sinner-lover, Jesus the best friend (and sometimes more disturbingly the boyfriend), Jesus the timid sort of mama's boy, or Jesus the joke, and every time we try to cast Him into one light, we are unintentionally limiting Him and His flexibility.

This is, I think, the first place in which Sayers rolls up her sleeves and gets down to work—her Jesus is vibrant and of many moods (like a human being! What makes us think that Jesus was in one mellow, pedantic mood at all times when we don't know a single person who operates consistently in the same box every day?). The first place we see her do this is in the notes concerning Jesus's voice. She says that unlike John Baptist, Jesus's voice has range and flexibility for "great fire and great gentleness." From the get-go, she desires to make us understand that Jesus is not some bookish character who plods from village to village (presumably causing miracles by accident, and in what would have to be some bewildering misunderstanding, ends up arrested for treason).

How could we have built this box for Him? What I like about this play is that Sayers helps us see that if Jesus were merely a mild-mannered rabbi with melted-chocolate eyes and nice moral teachings, there would be no reason for the Pharisees, as well as the government of Rome, to see a threat. And furthermore, what would attract an ever-increasing crowd of followers to someone so unremarkable? No, Jesus must be someone who speaks words of rebellion, who makes claims that in our day we would just as easily dismiss as heresy or lunacy. I love that we are challenged by this play to wonder if we would be someone with Sam Gamgee's following heart (like John Evangelist), or if we would look at this charismatic sensation with elegant cynicism, something for which American Christians seem to have a flair.

I see Sayers doing this throughout the play in the very scenes she chooses to include. She selects moments in which Jesus displays the gamut of human emotions—the bitter moment in which a son leaves His mother to become a man, the sense of humor with which He delights in Matthew, His strong sense of Judas's importance but His human limitation preventing Him from seeing what exactly lies ahead. I think Sayers is stressing that above every image we conjure for Christ, there is none as important as the fact that He lived, and He was human. And this dogma, that "he became flesh and made his dwelling among us," this is what she is bringing to life.

Lewis and Tolkien's View on Myth, and Myth Become Fact

by Christine Perrin

The theme, God dying and rising in history, which you have traced throughout these plays, is also cherished and articulated by C.S. Lewis and J.R.R. Tolkien. Here is a description of how two other Inklings described its importance.

At one point in his life, early in his relationship with Tolkien, Lewis saw myths as "lies and therefore worthless, even though breathed through silver,"[1] but Tolkien defended them as vehicles for truth. (He even wrote a poem for Lewis on the subject called "Mythopoeia.") Tolkien's answer was that they are not lies. At that moment in the conversation there was, Lewis wrote, "a rush of wind which came so suddenly on the still, warm evening and sent so many leaves pattering down that we thought it was raining. We held our breath."[2] Tolkien said about this scene:

> You look at trees . . . and call them "trees," and probably you do not think twice about the word. You call a star a "star," and think nothing more of it. But you must remember that these words, "tree," "star," were (in their original forms) names given to these objects by people with very different views from yours. To you, a tree is simply a vegetable organism, and a star simply a ball of inanimate matter moving along a mathematical course. But the first men to talk of "trees" and "stars" saw things very differently. To them, the world was alive with mythological beings. They saw the stars as living silver bursting into flame in answer to the eternal music. They saw the sky as a jeweled tent, and the earth as the womb whence all living things have come. To them, the whole of creation was "myth-woven and elf-patterned."[3]

Tolkien argued that knowledge and seeing means moving beyond knowing what stars are made of (flaming gas), and because of our fallenness and finitude we can only do this through the imagination with image, metaphor, and myth. Lewis's response to this statement was to wonder whether or not we create Christianity because we want to believe in something like it. This is how Freud viewed religious conviction—something we make up because we desire it to be true; he called it "wish fulfillment." Tolkien responded by asking, "Whence came the wish and whence the power to dream?" In other words, if materialist philosophy about myth is true, why do we even have these desires and wishes? What (or Who) gave us this longing and the joy itself? Tolkien forced Lewis to consider that, as Alan Jacobs puts it, "it was not Joy itself but its presence in a biological organism comprising largely water, nitrogen and carbon that constituted the greatest puzzle. That we dream and wish *at all* is a powerful element of the case for belief that myths communicate some truth that cannot be communicated any other way."[4]

---

1. Humphrey Carpenter, *The Inklings* (New York: Ballentine Books, 1978), 46.
2. Carpenter, *Inklings*, 46.
3. Carpenter, *Inklings*, 46.
4. Alan Jacobs, *The Narnian: The Life and Imagination of C.S. Lewis* (New York: HarperSanFrancisco, 2005), 145–146. For an excellent summary of this book, download the Mars Hill interview of Jacobs with Ken Myers at https://marshillaudio.org/catalog/alan-jacobs-narnian.

The craving for myths suggests the presence of a need they satisfy or try to satisfy. They reach something deep within us; because they do not and cannot meet the need they invoke, our experience with them is characterized by longing. The Christian myth is distinguished from the other myths in the sense that it is the true fulfillment of them—the enactment of their foretelling. It was a historical event versus an imagined story. Lewis wrote this about his evening spent with Tolkien and Dyson on Addison's Walk:

> Now what Dyson and Tolkien showed me was this: that if I met the idea of sacrifice in a Pagan story I didn't mind it at all: and again, that if I met the idea of god sacrificing himself to himself . . . I liked it very much and was mysteriously moved by it again, that the idea of the dying and reviving god (Balder, Adonis, Bacchus) similarly moved me provided I met it anywhere *except* in the Gospels. The reason was that in Pagan stories I was prepared to feel the myth as profound and suggestive of meanings beyond my grasp even tho' I could not say in cold prose "what it meant."
>
> **Now the story of Christ is simply a true myth: a myth working on us in the same way as the others, but with the tremendous difference that it really happened:** and one must be content to accept it in the same way, remembering that it is God's myth where the others are men's myths: i.e. the Pagan stories are God expressing himself through the minds of poets, using such images as He found there, while Christianity is God expressing himself through "real things." [bold added][5]

Lewis believed that all the stories that spoke of dying gods were anticipating (without knowing it) the fact of the dying God in the person of Christ. He believed that deeply lodged within us is an unconscious knowledge of such a Savior and that knowledge spanned centuries anticipating the factual arrival in time and space of Christ. Likewise, he believed that the Christian story partakes of the tradition of myth and storytelling and uses the power of that genre in seeking to speak powerfully to the human psyche to reveal God to the world.

> Now as myth transcends thought, Incarnation transcends myth. The heart of Christianity is a myth which is also fact. The old myth of the Dying God, *without ceasing to be myth*, comes down from the heaven of legend and imagination to the earth of history. It *happens*—at a particular date, in a particular place, followed by definable historical consequences.[6]

5. Jacobs, *Narnian*, 148–149.

6. C.S. Lewis, "Myth Became Fact" in *God in the Dock* (Grand Rapids: Eerdmans, 1970), 66.

Notes

Notes

WALKING TO WISDOM

LITERATURE GUIDE SERIES

Stories give us an experience of certain knowledge, which is why how we feel about the book is part of what the book is teaching us. We have kept this in mind while making the Walking to Wisdom Literature Guides, to be used in conjunction with the works of C.S. Lewis, J.R.R. Tolkien, and Dorothy Sayers. Each literature guide both stands on its own and interacts with the others, with sidebar comments and thematic continuity. These books will change students' lives and, in the meantime, teach them how to read with delight, depth, and skill.

Our literature guides thoughtfully instill students with the following habits:

- taking notes in their books
- answering reading questions and creating their own questions
- keeping notes book-wide on themes and motifs
- answering discussion questions about thematic material
- memorizing important quotations
- preparing, while reading, to write
- participating in creative enrichment activities related to the books

> "I believe that a large part of the value of reading great books is wrestling with the ideas and stories, and this series seems to be one of the best I've ever seen for accomplishing this." —Cathy Duffy

www.ClassicalAcademicPress.com